Contemporary
American Folk Artists

Also by Elinor Lander Horwitz

The Strange Story of the Frog Who Became a Prince
The Soothsayer's Handbook—A Guide to Bad Signs and Good Vibrations
Communes in America: The Place Just Right
Capital Punishment, U.S.A.
Mountain People, Mountain Crafts
When the Sky Is Like Lace

Contemporary American Folk Artists

ELINOR LANDER HORWITZ
J. Roderick Moore, Consultant

with photographs by Joshua Horwitz

J. B. Lippincott Company / Philadelphia and New York

The photograph of William Edmundson's *Jack Johnson* on p. 17 is reprinted from *Visions in Stone: The Sculpture of William Edmundson,* by Edmund L. Fuller, with permission of the University of Pittsburgh Press.

U.S. Library of Congress Cataloging in Publication Data

Horwitz, Elinor Lander.
  Contemporary American folk artists.

  Bibliography: p.
  Includes index.
  SUMMARY: Briefly discusses the lives and works of twenty-two American folk painters, carvers, and environmentalists.
  I. Horwitz, Joshua.   II.   Title.
NK808.H63   745'.092'2   75–14353
ISBN–0–397–31626–7   ISBN–0–397–31627–5 (pbk.)

This book is for my sister, Reyna.

Acknowledgments

Miles Carpenter, Uncle Jack, and Charles Gleason are represented by the American Folk Art Company, Richmond, Virginia.

Ralph Fasanella is represented by Jay K. Hoffman and Associates, New York, New York.

Sister Gertrude Morgan is represented by E. Lorenz Borenstein Galleries, New Orleans, Louisiana.

Inez Nathaniel is represented by Webb and Parsons Gallery, Bedford Village, New York.

Elijah Pierce is represented by Carolyn Jones, Columbus, Ohio.

James Rexrode is represented by the American Folk Art Shop, Washington, D.C.

Mario Sanchez is represented by Major Louise V. White, Key West, Florida.

Edgar Tolson is represented by the Pied Serpent Folk Art Gallery, Bloomfield Hills, Michigan.

The author also wishes to thank the following people for their advice and assistance: H. Parrott Bacot, Anglo-American Art Museum, Louisiana State University; William A. Fagaly, New Orleans Museum of Art; Edmund Fuller; David Haywood; Herbert W. Hemphill, Jr.; Carol Hopf, Pennsylvania Farm Museum of Landis Valley; John Irwin, Museum of Appalachia; Allan Jaffe, Preservation Hall; Mary Lou Kelley, *Christian Science Monitor;* Harry Lowe, Smithsonian Institution; Lynda Roscoe; Mr. and Mrs. G. A. Settle, Cedar Bluff, Va.; Bradley Smith, Heritage Plantation; C. Michael Smith, Southwestern Virginia Community College.

Contents

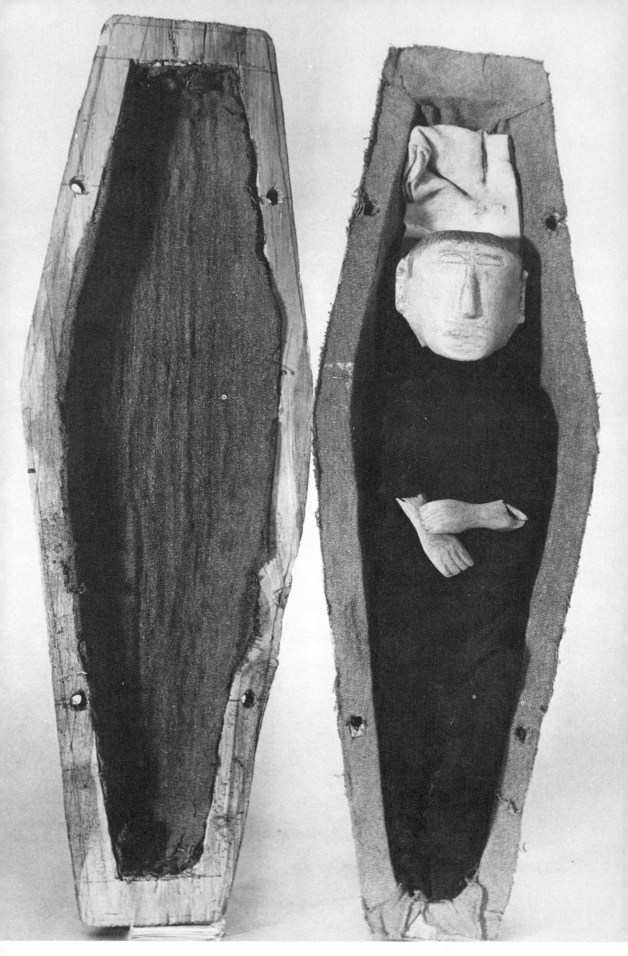

What Is Folk Art?

It is hardly surprising that arriving at a definition of folk art presents a problem, since until recent decades the old folk paintings and sculptures—rude wood carvings, primitive portraits and landscapes, stylized mourning pictures, samplers and inn signs, weather vanes and whirligigs—were simply not considered "art" at all. Ships' figureheads, wooden Indians, decoys, and scrimshaw were viewed as "quaint," "amusing," "historically interesting artifacts," but serious critics, art historians, and collectors directed their attention to "real" art—or what is commonly referred to as *fine* art.

Today American folk art is highly valued and eagerly sought by the most discriminating collectors and connoisseurs. Chic critics and erudite art historians proclaim its importance and analyze its allure. Savvy dealers and appraisers unhesitatingly laud the "investment potential" of a purchase of a vigorously carved eagle or a painting of a solemn husband and wife seated rigidly in Windsor chairs. The nonelitist art made by the common people for the use and pleasure of common people—rather than for a cultivated minority—has come into vogue. Folk art museums and special folk art exhibitions draw enthusiastic visitors of all ages who respond with unselfconscious pleasure to the charm, vigor, and ingenuity of the objects on display. The classics professor who worships Praxiteles; the art student who favors Matisse, Magritte, and Miró; and Grandpa, Susie, and Uncle Bill—who never heard of any of them, and who think that "art" is a bore—stand side by side, smiling with delight, in front of a tall painted wood carving of Uncle Sam.

If you interrupted their enjoyment by asking them to tell you what folk art *is*, you would probably find them equally at a loss for an answer. It's the big Uncle Sam, isn't it? Anyone knows that—and of course, that's true. And it's the flat painting of a strangely adult-looking child holding a rose, isn't it? That too. And if you're looking for a modern example, how about that carving by Kentuckian Edgar Tolson—the one of the man with the

11

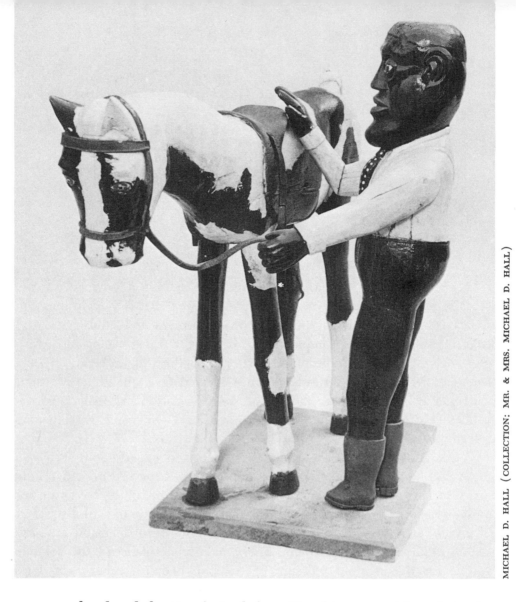

MICHAEL D. HALL (COLLECTION: MR. & MRS. MICHAEL D. HALL)

enormous head and the tiny feet who's patting his pony with such tender concern?

Most people can take pleasure in looking at folk art without worrying themselves about the question of definition, but authorities on the subject debate enthusiastically in books, at seminars, at exhibitions. The question "What is folk art?" is really three questions: What are the criteria of style and technique that make a given piece a work of folk art? What categories of objects make up our folk art heritage? What is twentieth-century folk art?

In the preface to the book *The Flowering of American Folk Art (1776–1876)*, folk art authority Jean Lipman suggests the common denominators of folk art as: "independence from cosmopolitan, academic traditions; lack

12

of formal training, which made way for interest in design rather than optical realism; a simple and unpretentious rather than sophisticated approach, originating more typically in rural than urban places and from craft rather than fine art traditions."

Other definitions are as sprinkled with negatives as a Christmas pudding is with raisins. We are told that folk art is *not* fine art, that it exists in an entirely different realm. It is *not* categorized either by "movements" or by "schools," since each folk artist makes his own rules. The highly individualistic folk artist has usually *not* been influenced by the trends, fads, and fashions of academic art and may be totally unaware that such movements exist. It is important to note that, although folk artists have generally been uninfluenced by the work of academic artists, in recent times the reverse has been quite a different matter. Since the 1920s many major artists have consciously studied and imitated the direct and crude—"childlike"—style of the folk artist.

What they are imitating are the once disdained "inartistic" qualities which pervade the work of the unsophisticated self-taught painter: faulty perspective, emphasis on pattern and detail rather than on accurate form. In the work of the folk artist colors and details are not dulled by distance; people may be larger than houses, background figures may be taller than those in the foreground, human and animal forms may be strangely misproportioned. The folk artist is unconcerned with conventional rules of composition and does not strive for realistic representation. And yet the best folk art has a powerful emotional insight and a startling expressive beauty. "Beauty" is a word rarely used in all the patter about definition, and yet it is the common denominator of all the arts. An object with no aesthetic appeal would merely be a folk "thing"—curious, perhaps, but not to be confused with art. The enjoyment of folk art depends to a great extent on knowing what to look for—not technical proficiency but vitality, strength, individuality, design.

American folk art is a home-grown product. An artistically talented young man born into an educated family in Boston or New York or Philadelphia in the eighteenth or nineteenth century was commonly sent to London or Paris to study painting. An equally gifted young man born into a poor family or in a rural community or on the frontier taught himself how to paint or carve, guided by his creative impulses and his personal vision. Because he was innocent of notions about the "correct" way to create a painting or a piece of sculpture, he went his own route, using whatever materials were available—buckeye rather than marble, house paint rather than oils. He recycled discards and imaginatively incorporated junk of all sorts into his constructions. Like the folk artists of today he did not refer to his creations as "art" or to himself as an "artist." Most often his work was unsigned because the idea simply never occurred to him.

Many people who write about folk art and artists feel that the term *folk art* more accurately denotes the traditional arts and crafts of certain European peasant cultures, and they prefer alternative designations. Because folk art is spontaneously and innocently rendered, it is often called "naive art," a usage generally preferred to "primitive art." One reason for this is that art historians have already usurped the label "primitive art" to mean either tribal art or the art of pre-Renaissance Italy. Folk art collector Herbert W. Hemphill, Jr., whose particular interest is in contemporary folk artists, sees the naive art of the past and that of the present as a continuum. He discusses terminology in this light in the introduction to his book, *Twentieth Century American Folk Art and Artists,* saying that today's folk artists, like yesterday's, ". . . participate in an art tradition that is timeless in its vision, attitude and content, and in various styles and techniques. If the word 'primitive' is to be applied to folk art it should be in the context of 'beginning' for the folk artist of every generation of every era begins anew the origin of art, over and over."

When we leave the subject of style and technique and move on to that of scope, controversy is rampant. To one critic, a carved wooden decoy is indisputably folk art; to another, the fact that many decoy carvers repeated a design over and over means that their products must be classified as craft, along with such other handmade "production" items as baskets or bean pots. Art, to most people, implies one-of-a-kind. Carousel figures and carved circus wagons are often classified with folk art, yet the carvers went through apprenticeship training and worked under supervision in carving factories. Most writers on the subject agree that a true folk artist must be self-taught; his work must spring from his own imagination. Folk art exhibits often include hooked rugs and patchwork quilts, but certain purists hold that anything made to serve a useful purpose is craft rather than art. Others hold that a utilitarian object may become art because of the aesthetic appeal of its decorative embellishments.

One characteristic of twentieth-century folk art, in comparison with earlier work, is the disappearance of the self-taught professional folk artist and the type of work he created. Early folk artists were of two types: the amateur, who worked at carving or painting for pleasure in his spare time; and the self-taught professional, who traveled around the countryside painting portraits of the farmer and his wife, the shopkeeper, and the country doctor; decorating walls and mantels; making inn signs or trade signs. The amateurs never expected to sell their skills; the professionals were paid in money or barter, and produced a vast quantity of the objects treasured by collectors today.

Although the thesis of this book is that American folk art is alive and well in the last quarter of the twentieth century, a number of writers have defined folk art as a product of the preindustrial, predominantly rural society which no longer exists. They cite the disappearance of certain *forms* of folk art, most of them practiced by the self-taught professionals of the first hundred years of the American republic. Certainly, many widely practiced specialties *have* died out. Gravestone carvings today are standardized and uninteresting; the introduction of the daguerreotype in the mid-nineteenth century brought an end to the wide demand for painted portraits; the huge trade signs which portrayed the product or service offered by a shop to a largely illiterate populace are increasingly difficult to find. Carved figureheads went out with the clipper ships, and farmers seldom make their own weather vanes. Original needlepoint pictures became rare when designs started being stamped on canvas, and it's been many a year since sailors scratched out scrimshaw drawings on whales' teeth.

And yet folk painting and folk sculpture are flourishing, and even some of the old forms are by no means entirely extinct. Although the cigar store Indians which once marked every tobacconist's shop have been retired to museums and private collections, and the once commonplace oversized watches and boots and eyeglasses and keys—and even the three hanging bronze balls of the pawnbroker—are now seldom seen, other trade signs remain. Barber poles are still with us and colorful palmists' signs are often seen; here and there a huge coffeepot tops a cafe or a monstrous horse guards a Western gear store. The small town of Wytheville, Virginia, boasts a striking trade sign. The old handmade wooden barber pole is overshadowed by a huge new pair of scissors which open and close, driven

by a motor. This arresting Creole cook modeled in concrete offers goodies on top of a restaurant just south of Natchez, Mississippi.

And speaking of portraits, it becomes more and more apparent that, although people no longer hire itinerant limners to paint their likeness, folk artists are still challenged by the idea of painting or carving—for their own satisfaction—the image of a well-known figure, a friend, neigh-

16

bor, or relative. This arrangement in gray and black—a lovingly rendered portrait of the artist's mother—was painted by a former bantamweight boxer, mechanical engineer, and cosmetologist named Alexander Bogardy, who lives in a basement apartment in Washington, D.C., three blocks from the Capitol. William Edmundson of Tennessee, who worked only in limestone, carved this blocky, rude, and powerful portrait of boxer Jack Johnson.

OSHUA HORWITZ   ROGER C. HAILE (COLLECTION: EDMUND L. FULLER)

Groucho Marx was rendered by an unknown New Jersey artist who used hair, wire, glass, painted stones, and plaster. Edward Kay of Michigan carved a totem pole from a pillar that had been in a hotel lobby. Gerald Ford is top man, followed by Rockefeller, Kissinger, and Richard Nixon—who sees and hears no evil. In the nineteenth century the favorite subject

17

C. MICHAEL DEPUNTE (COLLECTION: HERBERT W. HEMPHILL, JR.)

KENNETH FADELE

for portraiture was George Washington, and he's still popular today. Critics have written about similarities between some folk painting and children's art. Compare this wax crayon portrait of Washington by a five-year-old boy with Dow Pugh's portrait of Theodore Roosevelt (p. 112).

Although the forms of folk art have altered, the fact is that out in the country, up the hollow, and in big city apartments gifted but untutored men and women are working in the same tradition as their predecessors of a century or two ago. Some find inspiration in recent events; others in memories of times past. Most often the memories are of happy occasions or of everyday events which have acquired a patina of ease and pleasure.

In viewing folk artists as chroniclers it becomes apparent that, since their painting or carving often serves as an escape from an unfulfilling reality, they are highly selective in what they choose to record. Others find a rich source of inspiration in religion—in mystical visions, in the familiar stories of the Old and New Testaments. Like many folk artists, wood carver Edgar Tolson has rendered numerous scenes of the Garden of Eden.

JOSHUA HORWITZ
(COLLECTION: MR. & MRS. J. RODERICK MOORE)

COURTESY OF THE LOUISIANA STATE MUSEUM

What is the scope of folk art today? It is as broad as man's imaginings. It is the polka-dotted house of Creek Charlie, the ingenious root carvings of Miles Carpenter, the mystical paintings of Sister Gertrude Morgan. Contemporary folk art embraces such oddities as this imaginative walking stick carved out of walnut by Appalachian miner Ross Rutherford; lean on the head of the cane, and the monkey, dressed in a coat of cotton toweling, will raise his legs and his tail, point his gun, and lick his lollipop. It includes this magnificent creation of beadwork, sequins, and ostrich feathers made and worn as part of an annual folk festival—the Mardi Gras celebration in New Orleans. Bo Dollis, chief of the black "Indian" tribe known as the Wild Magnolias, made this costume himself in 1971 and posed for this photograph. Dollis explains that the costume must be newly made each year and that it becomes ever more elaborate. "I couldn't wear this one on the street in 1975," he says proudly. "Now I use a whole different design with rhinestones in place of sequins. The rhinestones are sewn on the sleeves, on the pants—on places you can't even see!"

The limited selection of folk artists whose faces and thoughts and work appear in the following chapters is subjective and in no sense comprehensive. Producers of only utilitarian items were specifically exempted. The artists included come from very different backgrounds. Some are urban; some rural. Some have roamed; others never left home. Almost all are elderly, and of these, most took up painting or carving after retirement or when the loss of a beloved spouse or parent left a void that seemed impossible to fill in the course of their daily routine. A number of these artists are capable, conventional people; many are markedly eccentric; a few may be intellectually impaired. The majority seem isolated in both the physical and spiritual sense. Some seem as innocent of standards for self-criticism as they are of standards of fine art, and they often take pride in pieces of work of very unequal quality. Many of the folk artists in this book use homely tools and materials—boards, house paint, car paint, penknives, wax crayons, found objects, tinfoil, broken crockery. Sister Gertrude Morgan uses this bone stylus for painting the eyes on her faces. Others have discovered and enjoy good quality brushes, oils, acrylics, and other tools of the professional.

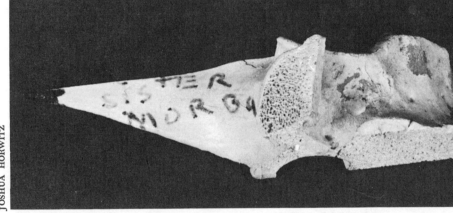

JOSHUA HORWITZ

The folk artists of former times came from a wide range of vocational backgrounds, and so do the living folk artists in this book. There are carvers who have worked in related crafts such as carpentry—yet the roster also includes a retired policeman, a retired fireman, a migrant picker, a barber, an antique dealer, a former schoolteacher, a street preacher, a fur salesman, a janitor. All of these men and women have been stirred by creative longings and the urgent need to express them. They took up art for the personal satisfaction it conveyed, and, although several now receive high prices for their work, none began with the motive of material gain.

The total environmentalists are people for whom a very private vision became an obsession, and the desire to create found an outlet in a project of enormous scope which took years—even decades—to fashion. Although the desire to leave a mark on history is not a common characteristic among folk artists, the three most important environmentalists in this book—Charlie Fields, James Hampton, Simon Rodia—were possessed by a passion to create a great work of art, a masterpiece unlike anything that had ever been made before. Although the book centers on living artists, these three men have been included because of their extraordinary interest. Each fashioned a splendid and unique environment. They cannot speak for themselves—and in each case considerable mystery obscured their motives when they were still living—but their wondrous and totally individualistic imaginings are hauntingly manifested in their art.

Why do folk artists create? They create because they are driven by the same impulses that lead all artists to seek a means of expression. They participate in the same creative joy as their more sophisticated brothers. They see the same visions. A story is told of Rodin that when asked how he carved a hand out of a block of marble he replied, " I don't make the hand—it's there inside. I just cut away everything that *isn't* hand." Miles Carpenter, who runs a rickety icehouse and watermelon stand in southern Virginia, has carved a grand fifteen-foot snake from the limb of a tree, and he will

readily tell you why and how he did it. "I saw the limb lying on the ground, and there was the snake—right inside! What I did is, I let him out!"

Few folk artists seek fame, and many speak deprecatingly of their work. They tell you it's "just whittlin'," "just something to pass the time." And yet others have the overwhelming sense of destiny that has stirred the greatest geniuses of the ages. William Edmundson, who lived in Nashville, Tennessee, until his death in 1951, was an unlettered man who worked at a variety of humble jobs. In his fifties he began carving, and, with a feverish devotion and intensity, he made hundreds of limestone figures. He had no problem explaining to people why he did it:

"These here is miracles I can do. Can't nobody do these but me. I can't help carving. I just does it. It's like when you're leaving here and you're going home. Well, I know I'm going to carve. Jesus has planted the seed of carving in me."

Folk Painters

Sister Gertrude Morgan

A hand-painted sign tacked to a porch post of Sister Gertrude Morgan's modest white house says EVERLASTING GOSPEL MISSION. From the house to the street the narrow front yard is completely carpeted with four-leaf clovers. Although her neighbors' garden patches in this drab ghetto area of New Orleans bristle with predictable assortments of substandard shrubs, desiccated grasses, and coarse weeds, Sister Gertrude regards the remarkable horticultural event that has taken place outside her own door without astonishment. Since her life has been marked by repeated instances of divine intervention, she views the unlikely greenery as further testimony to her very special and intimate relationship with the deity.

"It was just a lot of dirt out here, and I said, 'Lord, let what will grow just grow,' and the next thing, it come up like you see." She peers down at the clover, which gleams deep green in the summer sun. "Praise Him, praise Him, praise Him—halleluiah!" she sings out suddenly in a powerful voice. She turns and walks briskly toward the door. "Come on in. I don't have no time for sittin' on the front porch."

Sister Gertrude Morgan, robust and joyous and brimming with celebration of life at the age of seventy-four, is a former street preacher, a stirring gospel singer, a unique and gifted folk artist. In the stark front room where she delivers sermons and instruction, she sits on a white chair behind a table with a white cloth. The walls of the room are whitewashed. Sister Gertrude herself has dressed entirely in white since 1956, when, as she explains, she was wed to the Lamb. " 'Dress ye in fine white linen,' the Book says." The small folded handkerchief bobs on her head as she repeats the commandment. When she leaves home she wears a white cap with a chin strap. The room has seats for visitors—a collection of old wooden and metal chairs—and they too are painted white, with seat covers made of sheeting. On the wall a sign reads: "Christ is the head of this house, the unseen host at every meal, the silent listener to every conversation. Missionary Morgan, prophetess."

Sister Gertrude's obsession is communication, and she has spent most of her life zealously spreading the word of the Lord through every medium available to her. She preached and sang the gospel on street corners for almost four decades. Fifteen years ago she began to paint. Her visions of biblical scenes, enriched and adorned by written personal messages and New and Old Testament quotations, emerged in wax crayon, dime store paints, tempera, and, later—through the assistance of interested admirers—acrylics. She has painted, when the spirit moved her, on paper, on lamp shades, on cardboard, on toilet paper rollers (inside and out), on the plastic trays supermarkets use for packaging meats. She has applied her colors with brushes, sticks, a piece of bone worn to a point, a ball-point pen.

Although her work has made her famous in the small world of contemporary folk art experts, she is quick to disclaim any particular talent. "When I was a little girl I was always trying to draw something. I used to draw on the ground with a stick. Then sometimes I had a pencil or a crayon and some paper. One day I drew a mountain and a' train, and I was in the train waving, and my momma said, 'That girl is goin' to go far away from here'—and she was right." When she started to paint in earnest fifteen years ago she did so because of her conviction that it was God's wish. Paintings, she explains, are just another way of spreading the word. "He moves my hand," she says. "Do you think I would ever know how to do a picture like this by myself?"

God first spoke to Sister Gertrude on the thirtieth day of December in 1934. "We were living in Columbus, Georgia. It was a cold night—I remember that—and I was sittin' by the stove, and suddenly God called me. I'll tell you what He said." She draws herself up to a more noble posture, and her voice drops to a lower pitch. " 'Go ye in yonder's world and sing in a loud voice.' That's what He said to me. And then Jesus spoke to me and He said, 'Take up the cross and follow me.' " She shakes her head in wonder. "And so that's what I did. First I went to Montgomery, where the Lord told me to preach the gospel on the streets. Then I went to Mobile. I was in Mobile preaching and singing on the street corners when the Lord told me to come to New Orleans. I thought then that after New Orleans He was going to send me to California, but I never got there." She nods solemnly. "That must of been my addition, because this was the onliest California He gave me."

Sister Gertrude preached on the streets of New Orleans until she was sixty-nine years old. "Then God stopped me goin' out. He told me to stay indoors and pray and teach." She reaches for a megaphone—a plastic bleach bottle with the bottom cut away. She lifts it by the handle, puts the neck of the bottle to her mouth and sings: "I am the living bread, I am that bread. Eat this bread, you'll live forever. I am that bread." Her amplified voice echoes in the small room.

It's difficult to keep Sister Gertrude talking about painting, because preaching is her most compelling mission. "When I started to paint, the first things I did were about Daniel's dream of the four beasts that represent

JOSHUA HORWITZ (COLLECTION: THE AUTHOR)

the four nations." The second beast looms rich brown against a pink, yellow, and blue sky. She has painted other Old Testament scenes, but virtually all her recent work is based on the Book of Revelations, and particularly on the twenty-first chapter—John's vision of the New Jerusalem. Most of the time Sister Gertrude is in the picture as well. The New Jerusalem appears over and over again—here in wax crayon as a large building filled with small cubicles. Sister Gertrude and her bridegroom are to the left. In another picture made with wax crayons, she is wed to both God and Jesus. In a number of paintings titled *Jesus Is My Airplane,* she and her red-haired groom soar over the New Jerusalem as pink- and brown-faced angels sing hosannas.

Most of the paintings are adorned with calligraphy, and the writing becomes an integral part of the design of the work. The paintings vibrate with color and with energy and joy. Like her singing, they are suffused with an irrepressible fervor. Furthermore, they work. They communicate all the devotion and sincerity and passion of Missionary Sister Gertrude Morgan.

JOSHUA HORWITZ (COLLECTION: SUSAN CRAIG)

JOSHUA HORWITZ (COLLECTION: WILLIAM A. FAGALY)

C. MICHAEL DEPUNTE (COLLECTION: HERBERT W. HEMPHILL, JR.)

In 1973, when her paintings were exhibited with those of Bruce Brice and Clementine Hunter at New York's Museum of American Folk Art, she refused to leave St. Bernard Parish to attend the opening. "I'm a missionary to Christ before I'm an artist. The Lord ain't telling me to get there," she told reporters. "His Kingdom is planted right here, and I have to be here with it."

Sister Gertrude gained further recognition recently when poet Rod McKuen illustrated his book *God's Greatest Hits* with thirteen of her paintings. Despite these triumphs, her interests remain otherworldly. She talks about the conflict of good and evil as portrayed in the Book of Revelations as she steps out on the porch carrying the tambourine with which she has always accompanied her songs. "Well, God created the heaven and earth, and then He said, 'Let us make man,' and by and by He decided to make me. Halleluia." She begins an insistent beat on the tambourine. "Praise Him, praise Him. All the little children. God is Love. Thank Him. Thank Him. All you little children, God is Love."

She drops her voice to a confidential pitch and says, "When God speaks to me, He talks in family fashion as if speaking to a neighbor. His voice is loud and heavy." She raises her shoulders proudly. "Loud and heavy like this"—and she assumes God's voice. "'Everyone has to stop their wickedness. Rich, poor, black, white. It's judgment day!'"

The late summer afternoon breeze stirs the four-leaf clovers. As the visitors depart, Sister Gertrude sits down on her front porch, beating her tambourine, and her voice is rich and gravelly and filled with life: "I am the living bread, I am that bread. Eat this bread, you'll live forever. I am that bread."

JOSHUA HORWITZ

Uncle Jack

He's been called "Uncle Jack" for so long and by so many people that it seems almost irrelevant to note that his name is John William Dey. He has no children of his own, but he enjoys letting the neighborhood boys fix their bikes in his garage. A group of them invented the nickname, he says. He is a retired policeman who lives in Richmond, Virginia, and he estimates that he's done 650 paintings in the twenty-five or thirty years he's been at it. His work has a distinctive hard, glossy finish. The secret is the medium— Tester's airplane paint. The paintings are a patchwork of landscape and dream—of remembered scenes overlaid with fantasy and humor.

Uncle Jack is a precise and meticulous artist with his own rigid aesthetic standards. "When I've finished with a painting, I put a bright light on it, and I go over the whole thing with a magnifying glass to see if anything's wrong. Sometimes a picture just doesn't look like it's level, and then I have to put something on to anchor it—something like a cow or a rabbit." He points to a painting on the wall. "It looked kind of lopsided. It's the inside of a living room, so I put a clock over the mantel to anchor it."

When he was eighteen, Uncle Jack spent a year working in a lumber camp in Maine. "That was back in 1933," he says. "I was crazy about it up there. I paint about it a lot—the outdoors and the old cabins and the

31

snow. We used to see moose and there was a garbage bear—that's an old bear whose teeth are all wore down, and he eats garbage. I painted lots of bears—garbage bears, honey bears, and others. This here painting I call *The Moose Who Came to Dinner and Stayed*. We were up in that cabin in Maine, and when we saw the moose outside we shot him and butchered him. He tasted fine."

Many of Uncle Jack's paintings are snow scenes. "When you paint a winter landscape you have to fill it all up because it's so bare—you have to put all the branches on the trees, and then you have to put something up front."

There are three rabbits up front in the painting of the moose who stayed. For a model he used the design of a rabbit on the lid of his wife's jewelry box. In this painting one is beige, one gray, one black. The muted scene is enlivened by the bright green shutters on the cabin, and the frame is painted an intense blue.

Uncle Jack wants it understood that the act of creation properly starts

MOOSE WHO CAME TO DINNER AND STAYED.   UNCLE

JOSHUA HORWITZ

with the frame. A tireless haunter of antique and secondhand shops, he has collected frames of all shapes and sizes. "Once you pick the frame, then you put in a piece of wood and start painting. At first I used to use oil paint with a little bit of house paint too, but now I like the airplane paint. I buy it in the model store. When I first started painting, I took an old man and I put him on a rocking chair with a whiskey jug in his hand and I called it *Wife's Away*." Uncle Jack still enjoys that joke.

"Early on I made a masterpiece. There was a cat up in a tree robbing a nest. There was a redbird ready to get the cat. There was a man fishing and I put in a deer feeding. There were fish on the bottom of the lake and fish jumping and a big swan and a possum up the tree. All the time I was painting this masterpiece, my wife was fussing, 'You're putting in too much. Stop putting in so many things.' She likes scenery. She keeps telling me, 'Don't put in all those animals. Just make it scenery.'"

One of Uncle Jack's large recent paintings shows Adam and Eve in the Garden of Eden. The lake is glassy blue, there are pine trees on the mountain, and a waterfall drops sharply into the middle of the lake. The tempter has become a red-haired woman with horns who is saying (the dialogue is written on the painting): "Please just try it. You will like it." On the apple tree a sign says FORBIDDEN TREE. Eve is exclaiming: "I can't believe I ate that whole apple. I just can't believe I ate that whole thing."

Uncle Jack has a house filled with frames and an imagination bubbling with plans. "In this Mexican frame I'm going to do a picture of the Rever-

end fishing, and there will be a moose and the old chicken house and a lake. I can see it in my head. You know, if you're painting and it's quiet, you finish one thing and the other idea is right there waiting. Sometimes I wake up at three o'clock in the morning and an idea has stepped into my mind. Here I am with close to eighty-four frames. In this big one I'm going to do a picture of Charlie Chaplin. In this one I'm going to do another masterpiece with everything in it. I'll put the Reverend slam bang in the middle and all the people around, and the animals and some crows and rabbits, maybe a moose, and the lake. You know, when I was a lumberjack I wanted to be the best lumberjack, and when I was a policeman I wanted to be the best policeman, and now I want to be the best painter. What I don't have isn't ideas—I don't have enough time to do them all."

34

Charles Gleason

JOSHUA HORWITZ

Not far from Uncle Jack's apartment there is a small corner store where they sell groceries and make a good hamburger. The soft-spoken man who works at the griddle isn't the owner. He's an employee who lives in the neighborhood and who paints, right there in the store, when things are quiet. Charles Gleason was a fireman for twenty-one years and seven months, and since then he's been working in the neighborhood store. As to the painting—that had nothing to do with his retirement.

"I've been doing it ever since I can remember. My mother and father died when I was a kid and I lived with my grandmother. I did a lot of painting, mostly automobiles and trains, but I had it all jumbled around different places and I gave most things away. Once I sold a picture of a bridge and got three dollars for it. It was painted on an old window shade. You see, it was such a long bridge. It was the Lee Bridge. I wanted to get the whole bridge into the picture, so the only way I could do that was to paint it on a long unrolled window shade."

Gleason, who has lived in Richmond all his life, has always liked trains and enjoyed painting them. The train painting, like the *Lee Bridge*, uses a window shade for a canvas. "My father built locomotives, but me—I worked for the fire department. I was the hose man because I never did have a driver's license. I used to do some things for the fire department—

35

like signs saying 'Have a Safe Christmas,' pictures of candle lights, and things like that. I used to paint on tablecloths—oilcloth, you know. On the back. I just always liked doing it. I go out and paint sitting on the sidewalk or at home or in the store and I don't worry about nothing else. I can't do people, never could. I do buildings and cars and trains mostly. When you set up to paint out on the street, people keep coming by and telling you how to do it, but I don't care. I just do whatever comes into my mind."

Gleason's paintings are bold and handsomely designed. Trains crisscross on their tracks; the *Titanic* sinks elegantly. "I had an idea I wanted a picture of the *Titanic* sinking, so I did it." The painting is an early one that

has survived Gleason's generous gift giving. The smoke coming from the stacks was painted on another canvas and then cut out and pasted on. Sometimes Gleason pastes a cloud onto a painting, sometimes a car in front of the house, as in this street scene. "When a picture looks kind of naked I like to put something else in it later," he explains. Currently he's working on a bold rendition of a black bull, which looms in sharp outline against bright green grass. He'd never done a bull before, but "A man asked me to do it. He raises them and it's for his place."

Gleason is a modest and reticent man, and he is embarrassed by the interviewer's comments about "love of painting" or the desire for self-expression or the relationship of art to dreams and fantasies. "I'm not an artist. It's just something I do," he says gently, turning to wait on a customer. "Just something to pass the between time."

ANTHONY HORW

Gideon Cohen

Gideon Cohen is a small wiry man with thick white hair who walks with the springy gait of an athlete. "Oh yes," he says, in the lingering accents of east London, "I was always very big for sports, and I've been moderate all my life and watched my diet carefully. Oh yes, I feel fine, but it's because I've taken care of myself."

Cohen, who took up painting ten years ago when he retired, has achieved a satisfying degree of local fame in the Boston suburb of Arlington. His paintings cover the walls of his modest home on the second floor of a two-family frame house. He has painted favorite buildings in Arlington, Cambridge, and Boston, and remembered English landscapes and the harbor at Ogunquit, Maine, and the faces of his grandchildren, but his most extraordinary paintings are those of flower gardens, a subject he has painted and repainted over the period of a decade with constant meticulous attention to detail.

"I was always very interested in farming, and that's how I came to this country as a young man. But when we moved into this house in 1923 I had given up on farming. I started my garden in back here instead, and I've kept it going all these years. Let me show you." From a kitchen window you can look down at masses of flowers of many varieties. On the side, by the driveway, are the vegetables—tomatoes, peppers, cucumbers, eggplants, cantaloupes. The summer flower garden is a tangled profusion of giant blooms. "I used to keep it more trim," says Cohen with a trace of apology. "The children in the neighborhood pick things. They walk through. You know how children are."

Gideon Cohen's flower paintings vividly express his love of growing things—and they are also the realization of a fantasy. "I always put the poppies in the center or just a little off center. I don't know why. They just seem to tie in everything. Do you see what I mean? I have them in the garden but of course they're not out now. They come out at the same

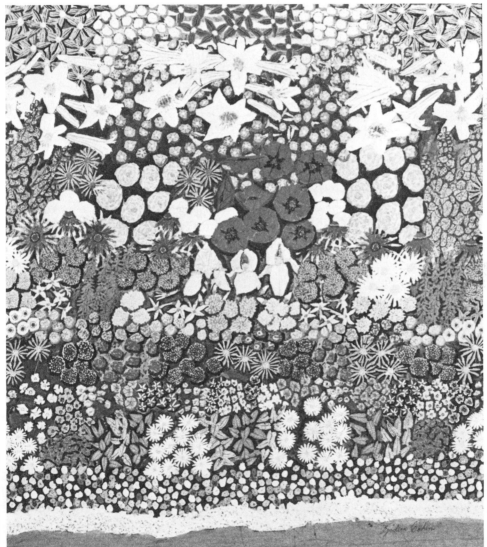

time as the irises and they make a wonderful show. My, they are splendid. In the paintings they're blooming with the irises and with the marigolds and the dahlias and the carnations and morning glories and clematis and zinnias and foxgloves and delphiniums and—well, that's the thing about painting. When you're making a garden, some things come out in June and some in August. When you're doing a painting, you can make all the flowers come out at once."

In the flower scenes the perspective works from bottom (near) to top (far), as it does in Persian miniature paintings. The jewellike colors and minute details are also reminiscent of Persian painting. The paintings, which vary considerably in size, appear similar at first glance, but they are far from identical. Near the lower edge there is always a border of alyssum, sometimes all white, sometimes blue and white. Above that the flowers are arranged in tidy clumps and rows, each one a perfect bloom. Every space is filled—with marigolds, flowering tobacco, dahlias, zinnias, Persian carpet zinnias ("they're entirely different from the others"), asters, gloriosa daisies, regal lilies, portulaca, verbena, salvia, carnations. He points to one flower painting—he calls them his "Floral Symphonies"—which is generously accented with tall spiky delphiniums. "I made them awfully thin—it's really not right, you know—but they just seem to look nice that way."

Cohen uses casein paints, and the kitchen table is his easel. "I was working in oil paints, and I still do sometimes, but another retired man I know— he took up painting because he was nervous and his doctor suggested it— he was using caseins on this illustration board—it's like a heavy cardboard —and I tried it and I like it too." In the past few years Cohen has won sixteen awards for his paintings. "It seems like a dream. I never even thought of painting until I retired and I was working in my garden all the time, and I thought I would like to try. I'd seen a man on television drawing in charcoal and I took a pencil and tried to draw the way he did, and that was the beginning."

During his London boyhood Cohen was too busy with work and sports to think about art. "My father was in the fur business and he was a real gypsy—always moving from one part of London to another. When I was a lad we lived for a while in Putney, and then later my father moved us to Dover. When we were in Putney I took to doing a lot of swimming in the Thames and I did long-distance walking. One day I hiked from Putney to Brighton. My father was going to be in Brighton, and I thought I'd meet him there and surprise him. I started walking early and I just walked the whole way—forty-six miles—and when I got there, he hadn't

40

come after all." Cohen chuckles at the memory. "I used to play a lot of cricket, and soccer too. I always liked sports—all sports, really."

When Gideon Cohen was twenty, he left England for Canada. "I had helped my father in the fur business, but in the summer I always worked on farms and that was what I liked most. The captain of a cricket team I was playing on liked farming too, and he told me about a wheat farm in Saskatchewan that needed young men to work, so I went over. It was in 1915 and things were bad. There was a real depression. I followed the crop south, but I couldn't make a living farming. After several years my uncle—he lived near Boston—asked me to come help him with his farm, but I just couldn't live on what I got in those hard times. The only other thing I knew how to do was furs, and after some years I went into the fur skin business. I used to buy raw skins from trappers, people in the country, men who had mink farms—places in Vermont, people all around north of here. I used to sell to retailers." He makes a gesture that indicates that all this was a matter of survival and had nothing to do with the pleasure and richness of life. "I always gave a good deal of time to

41

the garden. That took the place of farming for me. Let me show you where I have my compost."

Forty years ago Cohen and his wife went to England for a visit. "I had a camera and I took pictures in England. When I decided to try to paint, the first thing I did was to take those old pictures of England out of the attic and paint some of the scenes." He shows a painting of the Isle of Wight. "That's done from one of the English photographs."

A number of Boston and Cambridge buildings have attracted him strongly. He has painted interior and exterior views of the Isabella Stewart Gardner Museum in Boston and several houses and churches in Boston and Cambridge. "I did Trinity Church in Copley Square because I always

used to see all the artists out painting it, but I never knew why and I still don't. I never was crazy about it." Harvard University's Dunster House is another story. Cohen has painted it three times. Every line of the elaborately scrolled iron gate is perfect. "I'm very good at doing brickwork," he explains, "but when the leaves are on the trees, you can't see Dunster House. What I had to do is go and draw it when the leaves were off the trees. Then I came home with my drawing and I painted the building. When it was finished I put in the trees in front and I painted the leaves on them, but the whole building was already painted in behind them, you understand. Then I tried doing the gate on another paper first so I would get it right and not spoil the painting. I was very fussy with it. I always am. Very fussy."

JOHN C. GUILLET

Clementine Hunter

People could scarcely believe it was true when they heard that a new artist was turning out paintings at Melrose Plantation. Of course dabblers in watercolor and in oils were common enough at Melrose Plantation be-

43

cause the mistress, Cammie Henry, loved the company of cultivated and gifted ladies and gentlemen. She was an amateur painter herself and an enthusiastic patron of the arts. A procession of guests, many of them French-speaking and most of them "artistic," came to stay at Melrose for long periods of time. Poets walked in the garden by moonlight; musicians played in the drawing room after dinner; and there was always someone at work on a painting—but not in the kitchen.

Today, Clementine Hunter, the elderly illiterate black servant who spent almost seventy-five years in the fields, laundry, and kitchen at Melrose Plantation, has become more famous than the cultivated guests who spoke of Rodin and Michelangelo at the dinner table. In retrospect, she seems precisely the sort of woman whose abilities and experiences destined her to become an outstanding folk artist, although she was in her late sixties and many times a grandmother before her creative imagination led her to pick up a paintbrush. She was always a nimble-fingered and outstandingly capable woman. She liked everything she did to be done right and to look nice, and she always knew what "looking nice" was all about. She has always been praised for her cooking, her dressmaking, her handsome quilts, rag dolls, and decorations.

Her paintings are naive in execution, joyous, spontaneous, radiant with color. They depict all aspects of life in the rural South. Like so many folk artists, Clementine Hunter paints only happy memories. Even her funerals have an atmosphere of festivity. The women are wearing their best hats, the flowers are superb, the corpse rests in a sky blue coffin under a sunlit sky.

Clementine Hunter, who is now over ninety and twice widowed, paints the world she remembers. Her memories start back in the late nineteenth century, when she was a child at Melrose and at Little Eva Plantation up the road, alleged to have been the model used by Harriet Beecher Stowe for the plantation in *Uncle Tom's Cabin.* Clementine Hunter was born on Little Eva Plantation—then called Hidden Hill—and moved with her parents to Melrose at an early age. She has been there ever since. Her parents had been slaves, and her view of the world is bounded, as theirs was, by the unchanging landscape of northern Louisiana—the hot, flat Cane River country of Natchitoches Parish.

Her memory of the world begins with the cotton fields and pecan groves that she still sees today. "When I was a child I could pick two hundred and fifty pounds of cotton a day," she says. She has painted the pickers working under the hot summer sun. She is interested in their big hats and their full sacks—and not in perspective. The pickers walk in rows, one above

the other, the background figures larger than those in the foreground. She remembers what it was like when she went out to gather pecans on a cold morning, and a small wood-burning stove was brought into the groves. In her painting an old woman cooks biscuits and coffee for the pickers, a child carries the coffee cups, and a "gooster"—her own fanciful make-believe bird who combines the best qualities of a goose and a rooster—watches the scene with curiosity.

Clementine Hunter, who spent most of her life as a field hand, had become chief cook at Melrose by the time she began her career as a painter in the late 1940s. A Frenchman named François Mignon had come for dinner at the plantation many years before and had stayed on as a permanent guest. He wrote charming little literary and historic vignettes for local publications, and he was an elegant addition to the household. One night, the cook, who had noted the paints left out by a visiting artist from New Orleans, told Mignon that she thought she could "mark a painting" if she could use one of the brushes. In the morning Mignon found a gift outside his door, painted on an old, torn window shade.

Once she began painting, Clementine Hunter painted on everything she could find—cardboard, old pieces of used wrapping paper, empty bottles, shoe boxes. She painted the pictures she could see without even opening her eyes: a girl bringing slops to the hogs, women scrubbing the wash in big tubs under the trees, the church, the plantation house, gourd picking, weddings, funerals, a wild Saturday night at a roadside honky-tonk. She painted the Nativity, black angels dressed in white and red gowns floating through the air. She painted her feelings about people and nature. Old people are always treated with great respect in her paintings; women are almost always much larger—more important?—than men; flowers are enormous and are often rendered with paint piled up in an impasto technique to give them special prominence. In the world of her paintings everyone is black except Cammie Henry, who appears in the corner of a

47

large study of the plantation tending a flower garden. When asked how she decides on her subjects, Clementine Hunter says, "I just paint by heart."

Despite some stylistic experimentation, her subject matter has scarcely changed over the years. François Mignon encouraged her, provided her with paints, introduced her work to critics and collectors. He taught her how to sign her initials on her paintings, but in later years she reversed the C because "Mrs. Cammie Henry painted too, and I never felt good about having the same letters." Paintings from the early period are distinguished from later ones by this signature.

Clementine Hunter lived for some years in Africa House, a famous building on the plantation constructed in about 1800 by slaves who modeled it on their memories of a West African house. She painted murals for Africa House which are now in private collections. Today she is still living in a small cottage across the road from the main house of Melrose. Her home is heated by a wood-burning stove and has no indoor plumbing. A sign hanging in front says PAINTINGS FOR SALE. A number of proud Louisianians will tell you that Grandma Moses is "the North's Clementine Hunter."

Collectors of her paintings have insistently asked her to visit them in New Orleans, but she has refused to leave Natchitoches Parish. She has not attended any exhibitions of her work. "I ain't interested. I don't travel," she says emphatically. Her fans drive long distances to visit her and to buy paintings in which everyone is either working or celebrating while goosters gaze at flowers that are as large as trees. In her old age the artist has decided that painting is more difficult than picking cotton. "Cotton's right in front of you," she says, "you just have to pick it off the bush. To paint a picture you have to study your head."

James Rexrode

James Rexrode began painting at the age of seventy-eight, and he insists that when he decided to give it a try he had never seen anyone in the process of drawing or painting a picture. He is now eighty-six, and he still hasn't seen another artist at work. "I just don't know how they go about it," he says.

It's difficult to believe that a man who is living in an area relatively close to several small cities can make this statement, and yet James Rexrode has left Sugar Grove, the tiny West Virginia village in which he was born, only twice. On both occasions he had had a stroke and was rushed by his son to the hospital in Staunton, Virginia. Today he is no longer able to paint, having been left paralyzed and virtually blind as the result of these illnesses. He lives with his son, who is puzzled by the interest of outsiders in his father's paintings, a number of which are now owned by celebrated collectors.

Clementine Hunter, who also never left home, was exposed to men and women from distant states and countries who came as visitors to Melrose Plantation, and there were many artists among them. She was also fortunate in having had encouragement and material assistance from her sophisticated sponsor, François Mignon. But James Rexrode, living in an isolated community, cut off from easy access to nearby towns by mountains and poor roads, learned how to paint in his own way as American folk artists have done through the centuries. He simply used whatever materials he had at hand as he continued fashioning pictures of remembered scenes from his childhood. He used cardboard and Masonite and car paints, because they were available in Sugar Grove. There was considerable question in his mind about what the "proper" materials were in any case.

The inspiration for Rexrode's paintings was the beautiful green valley in which he'd spent his life. He was deeply concerned that his memories of the way things were done when he was young would be lost. There is no question about the fact that he regards himself as a chronicler, and he takes the job very seriously.

Because he painted scenes of old-time rural life, James Rexrode is often dubbed "Grandpa Rexrode" by people who link his work with that of the late Grandma Moses. Although no one would mistake the paintings of one for those of the other in a stylistic sense, both artists have painted detailed works which have value as archives of local history. Both have given scrupulous attention to how specific jobs were done: how people stacked their hay and made their apple butter and maple sugar, how they butchered hogs and went sleighing and danced when work was finished. In the worlds of James Rexrode and Clementine Hunter and Grandma Moses people work and work and work—under sparkling skies, in an atmosphere of serenity and contentment.

Rexrode's zest for accuracy may well be connected with the fact that, starting at the age of seventeen, he spent his life as a teacher. He taught first in the one-room schoolhouse where he himself had been a pupil. In the summer he farmed and raised sheep and milk cows. When he began to paint, he visited farmers who still had pieces of obsolete equipment in the barn, to check details of which he was no longer certain. He wanted, more than anything else, to leave an honest and instructive record of rural life in the early decades of the twentieth century.

When he was a child in the one-room schoolhouse in Sugar Grove, young James Rexrode tried one day to sketch the scene from the window on his slate. He remembers that he was soundly thrashed by the schoolmaster for his frivolity and inattention. He was apparently effectively discouraged.

BUTCHERING   J.T. REXRODE

His only other artistic activity before the age of seventy-eight came when, as a young man, he amused himself by making comic valentines which he mailed—unsigned—to people he admired.

When he began to paint in his old age he started with historic buildings in his region—churches, log houses and barns, old schoolhouses. His first success came when he painted the old Mount Hobeb Church, and thirty-four members of the congregation vied for the picture. James Rexrode, delighted with this sign of appreciation, sat down and painted thirty-three copies. After all, these were his neighbors!

Once Rexrode began, he worked at a rapid pace. He painted wash day, butter churning, a cider mill and press, skaters on the stream, people going to church, threshing and winnowing buckwheat, Christmas scenes, homecoming dinners, soap making, barn raisings, quilting parties. His colors are flat and strong. The South Fork Mountain, which forms the landscape he has viewed every day of his life, is often the backdrop for the work that

51

goes on and on—performed by people who knew who they were and what had to be done and how to do it, and who knew how to have fun when the job was completed.

JOSHUA HORWITZ

Hattie Brunner

When Hattie Brunner was a young woman, the autumn leaves in the Pennsylvania Dutch country turned red and orange and yellow and a particularly dazzling shade of bright blue which no one has seen in recent years. At least that's how she remembers them in her paintings.

Hattie Brunner, eighty-five years young, has been selling antiques for over half a century. Having started life in conditions of great privation, she became one of the most knowledgeable antique dealers in this part of the country. At the age of sixty-seven she also became a painter.

The scenes she remembers with the greatest delight are the old country furniture sales where she picked up some of her very finest pieces. In the paintings it is always autumn and everything is on display, spread out on the farmhouse lawn. Farmers and collectors and dealers like Hattie—whose eye for quality is considered impeccable—examine the lowboys, desks, dower chests, sawbuck tables, the fine quilts and coverlets.

"That's me," she says with pleasure, in the lilting singsong accents of the Pennsylvania Dutch. "I'm the one looking at the tilt-top table. That's Joe Kindig near the high-backed chair. Everybody knew him. He had long hair and a long beard and he was a famous dealer. Near the end of his life his hair and beard turned from dirty yellowish to totally white."

Hattie Brunner lives in the center of the tiny village of Reinholds, Pennsylvania, next door to the general store, in the house to which she came as a servant at the age of ten. She arrived with three years' experience, and the Brunner family was happy to have her. The fact that she would one day marry their son was not imagined at the time, but her

intelligence, capability, and industry endeared her to everyone. She had
been born two miles away on a small farm, and when her father died,
leaving her mother penniless and helpless, seven-year-old Hattie was sent to
live with an old woman. "She paid me one dollar a month and gave me
room and board, and I went to school and cleaned the house and cooked
and washed the dishes." She took on similar duties when she moved to
the Brunner household, and later, as a teenager, she also worked in the
family's store next door to the house.

Although most of her life has been spent in the big old house in Reinholds, there was a time when young Hattie Brunner left the tidy farms and
small villages of southern Pennsylvania and set off to seek her fortune. She
worked first as a waitress in Asbury Park and then went to Philadelphia
where she attended the Philadelphia Musical Academy. To earn her tuition
she worked for a milliner. "It was a very elegant hat shop," she remembers.
"All the trimmings came from France. We made the finest straw hats. I
made one once for Theodore Roosevelt's cousin, and it cost thirty-five
dollars—way back in those days!"

After she had been away for about five years, she returned home to stay. The Brunners' son had been left a widower when his young wife died in childbirth, and Hattie, then twenty-nine, became his second wife. "When I married him it was almost like marrying my brother. We were children in this house together, and I'd been at his first wedding, and it was real strange."

Hattie never had children of her own, but she adopted her husband's son and has spent her life surrounded by cousins, grandchildren, nephews, and nieces. Her mother- and father-in-law and a sister-in-law lived in the house until they died. Her husband died twenty-two years ago. Now a nephew runs the store next door, and Hattie Brunner lives in the house alone. She has been a member of the Swamp United Church of Christ for seventy-two years, and she was their organist for many decades. She does not go to movies, has never owned a television set or ridden in a plane. She dislikes travel.

The house is also her antique shop. It was from her mother-in-law, a collector of Pennsylvania Dutch furniture, that she first learned the business. One day, when she was sixty-seven years old, Hattie Brunner picked up a watercolor brush while baby-sitting with her grandson. "I had bought him the paint set to amuse him and he kept saying to me, 'Now, Grandma, you paint a picture.' So I started putting color on the paper, and I tell you, I was so enthused!"

The enthusiasm lasted. Hattie Brunner took time off from the house, the store, and antique hunting to work at her painting. "You take some color and put it next to some other color and it's so alive! They wanted to call me the second Grandma Moses, but I said, 'I'm Hattie Brunner!'" Her voice drops and she laughs. "Anyhow, I hear her work is a little more sloppier than mine."

Like Clementine Hunter and James Rexrode, she has chosen to remember in her paintings scenes that pleased her. "Everybody has a lot of stuff that's depressing," she says staunchly. "We just leave that out when we remember."

This painting of an old hearse is no exception. The snow shimmers and people head for the church wearing bright red coats. The painting hangs in the nearby funeral home of Mr. E. Louis Roseboro, who displays it with great pride. "This is my father-in-law at the reins of his horse-drawn hearse. Hattie saw it when she was a young girl, and we also had a photograph. My father-in-law was a very progressive man and he replaced it with a motorized hearse in 1915. When he died in 1964 I asked Hattie to paint this picture for us."

The Pennsylvania Dutch woman, who has worked hard every day of her life, is still busy. Her eighty-eight-year-old brother comes over for noon dinner and visits again in the evening, and she's working on an antique show in Ephrata, and she's far behind in the paintings she's promised to do for friends and relatives.

She accepts compliments on her youthful stride with obvious pleasure. "One eye doesn't see right, and I get worse-looking all the time, but as long as I feel well, I say the hang with the looks. The important thing is, I'm still in business. I'm still working."

MICHAEL D. HA

Inez Nathaniel

The people in Inez Nathaniel's drawings stare out at the world and at each other with wide, unblinking eyes. In profile the eyes also face front, like those of ancient Egyptians or Assyrians. The line drawings, done in pencil, colored pencil, and felt-tip marker, are bizarre and haunting. Who is this man—or is it a woman?—who rides the tiny bicycle and feeds a worm to a bird? Who is the man with the minute bow tie and the strangely decorative beard? Two young women, one black and one white, sit conversing, and there is an urgency about the gestures of the speaker's tiny hands and the attentive expression of the listener.

The artist explains that most of her drawings are "all about bad girls"— the girls she met during her confinement in the Bedford Hills Correctional Institution, New York's state prison for women.

"Lordy," she says, "a woman got to keep her head around her! There was all those bad girls talking dirty all the time, so I just sit down at a table and draw."

Inez Nathaniel, who has returned to migrant farm work in upstate New York, has continued to draw the bad girls and the inscrutable—sometimes androgynous-looking—men. They are "childlike" drawings that originated in the imagination of a mature woman, nurtured by the experiences of a harsh life. Born in Sumter, South Carolina, in 1911, she received minimal education and was married at the age of thirteen. She became the mother of four children and migrated north to Philadelphia, where she worked in a

pickle plant. From there she went to work as a picker in the apple fields of New York State.

While in prison from 1971 to 1974 she began to draw on the back of the mimeographed prison newspapers in the evenings and during a remedial English course. The English teacher took an interest in her doodlings, brought her drawing paper, and showed her work to the owner of a folk art gallery in Bedford Village, New York. The drawings have since been exhibited in group shows, in Bedford Village at the Webb and Parsons Gallery in 1972 and 1974, and in a show titled "Six Naives" at the Akron (Ohio) Art Institute in 1973.

In an interview with sculptor Michael Hall in 1973, which preceded the Akron show, she gave the following statement: "I just sit down and go to drawing. You know—the more I draw the better I get. I don't look at nothing to draw by. Just make 'em myself. I can't look at nobody and draw. Now that's one thing I wished I could do. But I can't. I just draw by my own mission, you know. I just sit down and start to drawing."

GEORGE PLATTETER

Ralph Fasanella

Ralph Fasanella is not a benign man. No one will ever describe his work as "quaint" or dub him "Grandpa Fasanella"—not even when he's very old. He is a restless and passionate artist whose paintings—inspired by his

60

personal history, his political and social ideals, and the nation's recent past —are filled with anguish and with a love that can almost be described as ferocious. He is a painter who burns with outrage at social injustice and who expresses himself vividly in language, in action, in his art. "The day I stop protesting," he says, "Ralph is finished. Dead."

He is not your usual folk artist. Not at all.

Although a great many academic painters have used their work as a means of exposing social or political wrong, this direction, as we have seen, is uncommon among self-taught artists. The folk painter or carver often takes up painting or carving to counteract pressing personal problems, dispiriting privations, or intolerable loneliness, or to create a world that reflects an obsessive fantasy life. His imagination sorts out his memories, rejecting disturbing subjects, evoking peaceful scenes which give him pleasure.

But then, to prove that generalizations are always risky, there is Ralph Fasanella, who infuses his work with a walloping emotional thrust. Fasanella is a short, stocky, chain-smoking, effusive, excitable urban man. His city is New York, and it is a New York crammed with buildings and lights and bridges and cars and people and color and noise and love and hatred. It is not entirely fanciful to say that you can hear the sounds of the city when you look at his paintings, because they are there.

Fasanella has been painting furiously for three decades. During most of that time he earned the major part of his income pumping gas in his brother's service station underneath the Cross-Bronx Expressway. He was born on Sullivan Street in Greenwich Village on Labor Day 1914, and he now lives outside the city, in Ardsley, New York, with his wife and two children. Since his discovery by a Manhattan agent in 1972, his name has become well known, and the prices of his paintings have soared. He has been given one-man shows and a cover story in *New York Magazine*. A book has been written about his life and his work.

Which is a long way from Sullivan Street. As one of six children of an Italian immigrant family, Fasanella had a childhood shaped by the rough reality of the slums—by poverty, ethnic rivalries, minor delinquencies. His father, who appears in many of his paintings, was an iceman who drove around the streets of New York in a horse-drawn wagon, selling ice in twenty-five-, fifty-, and one-hundred-pound blocks. At the age of eight Fasanella was working on his father's ice truck twelve hours a day, every day of the week.

His mother was a literate and intelligent woman who was dedicated to left-wing political causes, and the artist traces his own involvement to her influence. As a teenager he marched with her in demonstrations during the years when she worked in a buttonhole factory and helped edit a radical Italian-language newspaper. As a result of her persuasion he went to Spain to fight in the Civil War. He served in the U. S. Navy in World War II and then during his twenties worked as an organizer for the United Electrical Workers' Union.

Since he began to paint he has completed close to two hundred canvases, many of them very large—as much as seven feet in width. "A painting's no end, it's a beginning. It begins like life," Fasanella has said.

The paintings are as crammed and cluttered with detail as Brueghel canvases. You can look at them over and over again and make new discoveries. He has painted the Sullivan Street of his childhood and the Catholic Protectory in the Bronx, a reform school where he was sent three times as a child because of truancy and rebelliousness at home. He has painted the tenements, office buildings, and streets of New York in every season. He has painted his friends in the crowds at the annual San Gennaro Festival. Boys play stickball in the streets, demonstrators march, walls fall away to show the interiors of buildings, lights sparkle, signs are everywhere.

GERALD KRAUS

GERALD KRAUS

He has painted baseball players on empty lots and in stadiums and at the reform school. While the "good" boys play, the "bad" boys stand against the wall as punishment. He has painted the union hall with signs on the wall saying BE HAPPY GO UNION . . . JOIN TODAY . . . A MEMBER A DAY IS THE UE WAY. He has painted the exteriors and interiors of looming Catholic churches which gleam with ruby light. He has painted a vast canvas of a May Day parade of the 1930s with a platform displaying portraits of Sacco and Vanzetti, Roosevelt, Jefferson, Eugene Debs. He has painted the assassination of John F. Kennedy and titled it *American Tragedy*, and he has constructed two large complex paintings of the execution of Julius and Ethel Rosenberg.

Ralph Fasanella's father, dispirited by the endless toil of carrying heavy blocks of ice on his back up endless tenement staircases, deserted the family when the artist was fourteen. In later years the son came to view his father as a contemporary Christ, sacrificed to the frustrations and pain of unceasing backbreaking toil. Several canvases titled *Iceman Crucified* portray his father nailed to a cross. In one he hangs suspended by the ice tongs, which pierce his head. In the painting *Family Supper* (which the artist has

also referred to as *Last Supper*), the crucified iceman has become a small painting on the wall, a contemporary religious icon. The family sits at the table in the tenement kitchen crowded by a bed, a sewing machine, a large trunk from Italy. The mother stands tangled in children and clotheslines. There are stores below and neighbors on all sides and the ice wagon is parked by the sidewalk. "It's how we lived," the artist explains. On a bucket of ice in the corner of the room the words are inscribed: "In memory of my father Joe. The poor bastard died broke."

JOSHUA HORWITZ

Bruce Brice

Another highly productive self-taught urban artist whose work has attracted considerable attention in recent years is Bruce Brice, a thirty-two-year-old native of New Orleans.

The city in which he has always lived is the city Bruce Brice loves, and the subject of all his paintings. One week, in an unaccustomed mood of pastoral yearning, he painted himself seated at his easel on a hillside in

65

the country, surrounded by watermelons and farm animals. Brice, who lives in the old French Quarter of town, admits that he never leaves the city, but "That's the thing about painting. You can put yourself in a whole new place."

Bruce Brice grew up in the Quarter, where he shined shoes for nickels starting at the age of eight. His father ran a dice game at a gambling house and later owned a beer hall. He remembers his childhood as a happy time, and he's irritated when people challenge the festive and exuberant subject matter of most of his paintings.

"There's too much tragedy going on in the world," he says, and adds unapologetically, "I want to paint scenes in which people are having a good time."

His art portrays New Orleans as a city filled with music, dancing, unique customs. He paints the members of the neighborhood social aid and pleasure clubs, waving fans and umbrellas, dancing down the street behind the band dressed in their custom-tailored, brightly colored clothes. He paints parades and parties, Mardi Gras "Indians," the processions of elaborate floats. He paints jazz funerals and the old French market and friends

and neighbors: artists; jazz musicians; Buster Holmes, who runs the soul food restaurant on the corner of Burgundy and Orleans, where you can eat an enormous quantity of red beans and rice for forty cents. You can find Brice there almost every noon, enjoying his meal and visiting with friends, but the rest of the day, and much of the night, he's at his easel. He has worked at a lumberyard and in a coffee company, and at one time he made marionettes and gave puppet shows. He seriously considered a career as a professional puppeteer, and the influence remains. The street dancers in his paintings look more than anything else like frenzied marionettes whose stylized movements are controlled by invisible strings.

Brice always liked to draw and paint. In his twenties he began joining the sidewalk artists of Jackson Square on weekends, occasionally selling his work to passersby. During the past few years he has been painting full time. His paintings were exhibited in 1973 at New York's Museum of American Folk Art along with those of Sister Gertrude Morgan and Clementine Hunter. One of his paintings won a purchase award in the biennial competition at the New Orleans Museum of Art. Another of his paintings fills a page of the 1976 UNICEF calendar.

Although he began by painting a rather uninteresting series of portraits of jazz musicians, in recent years Brice has developed a style that is unique, personal, enormously engaging. His materials are most commonly acrylics on Masonite, although he also works in oil paints and occasionally in watercolor. His buildings, streets, skies, figures are painted in vibrant flat colors—turquoise, magenta, canary yellow, pink, lavender, spring green. Brice has a fine eye for design, and the shutters, iron balconies, leaves on the trees, cobblestones, patterns on fans and umbrellas are detailed precisely in black. Under sky blue skies his street dancers, with expressions of almost manic delight, dance on and on and on behind the Olympia brass band.

A painting of children playing became the model for the first of his three murals—this one for a recreation area. Soon afterward he painted murals on two opposite walls on St. Phillips Street in the old neighborhood of Treme, most of which was razed to provide space for a culture center.

Brice speaks with anger and regret of the passing of the old black neighborhood. "People lived here for generations, and plenty of them were old folks whose whole life was in the neighborhood. One of the social aid and pleasure clubs used to meet on this demolished corner, at the Caledonia. The Economy Dance Hall was a landmark; so was the San Jacinto Hotel and Dance Hall. In my mural all the people are leaving. They're being pushed out without being relocated." He points to the central

JOSHUA HORWITZ

Uncle Sam figure. "There's the long arm of the law saying: 'Out! We're replacing your old culture with *our* kind of culture.'"

One of Brice's most ambitious paintings hangs in a New Orleans architect's office. It is a city panorama with Jackson Square in the middle, Mardi Gras floats going down the street, and the Mississippi River in the background with barges carrying gravel and shells. The grand marshal leads the band, a king float makes the turn, and Buster—the restaurateur —serves Bruce Brice a big plateful of red beans and rice.

Like Fasanella, Brice spent his childhood immersed in the vitality, excitement, and danger of the city streets. Like Fasanella he is not a "naive" personality, and to some critics this is a disturbing characteristic in a folk artist. In talking about the work of men like Ralph Fasanella and Bruce Brice you come up against arguments about definition—and the emotional responses of purists who like their folk artists to be indisputably "folky."

Bruce Brice worked for years as a picture framer at an art gallery, where he was exposed to the standards of "fine art." He calls himself an artist and is trying very hard to support himself on the sales of his paintings. Furthermore, he's been painting for most of his adult life. Do these facts disqualify him as a folk painter? Certainly not.

A New Orleans art dealer and admirer of Brice's work disputes the notion that definitions of folk art cannot include a man who thinks of himself as an artist and is familiar with such names as Picasso, Renoir, Leonardo. Brice is a folk artist, he insists, because he paints the "folk" in a genuine folk style. "Take Joan Baez," he says. "When Joan Baez sings a folk song, everyone calls her a folksinger, but Joan Baez sure ain't folk!"

The young man from New Orleans is hopping with energy and ideas. Like many other folk artists he has finished a large canvas of Adam and Eve. Since he admires Sister Gertrude Morgan he has put her in the upper left-hand corner, striking the devil down with a thunderbolt and carrying a sign saying: "The time to do right is now. It's always time to do right." On the other side of the central figures, couples who have achieved eternal bliss swirl and float and dance in a sky filled with birds.

"Painting is what I want to do for the rest of my life," says the artist, who lives in the most colorful area of the most picturesque city in the

United States. The sounds of New Orleans fill his ears day and night. Up the street is Preservation Hall, where the best jazz musicians perform nightly. At the corner a bar hosts one band from one to seven P.M. and another from seven P.M. to one A.M. In the summer the long shutter doors of the bar are opened wide, and the children tap dance in the street for coins to the strains of "Bourbon Street" and "When the Saints Come Marching In." Half a block away Bruce Brice sits by his open window painting the New Orleans that is, the city that was, and scenes from his relatively recent boyhood that are gone forever.

JOSHUA HORWITZ (COLLECTION: MR. & MRS. J. RODERICK MOO
CARVING BY W. S. ROSENBALM

Folk Carvers

Miles Carpenter

The man who runs the old icehouse and watermelon stand in the center of Waverly, Virginia, enjoys his work. In the tiny town of Waverly, about an hour's drive south of Richmond, refrigerators have not yet totally replaced the old iceboxes, and the demand for twenty-five-pound blocks is still pretty brisk. A few grocery items are sold at the icehouse as well—bottled soft drinks, a varying assortment of fresh garden vegetables. When the season is at its height, ripe watermelons are stacked high. If you drive by and he's not there, just give a honk, and Miles Carpenter will come running over from his house, which is right next door.

JOSHUA HORWITZ

Miles Carpenter is a famous man. Collectors of contemporary folk art consider him one of the most versatile and imaginative carvers working today. To the local people, he's the old man who has always been there at the stand—a lonely widower who is delighted to stand and chat with you about the garden produce, the weather, your health, his health (splendid, thank you). If you're interested in talking about his extraordinary wood carvings, he'll accept the compliment with modest pleasure and give you the straight story on how to fashion a fine watermelon from a dead stump, a bullfrog from an old root, a snake from a tree limb.

Carpenter says he's eighty-five years old, but he looks at least a decade younger, walks with a vigorous step, drives his 1951 Chevrolet when he has errands to take care of. Good health, he says, runs in the family. His ninety-one-year-old brother, a registered surveyor, still tramps around the woods working at his job. "He mostly does small pieces of land now, not big pieces of acreage where you have to do a whole lot of climbing." On the subject of automobiles, he points to his trim blue Chevy and says, "I wouldn't take a new car for this one. They're not made as strong any more, you know. I drive around in the country all right, but since my wife died seven years ago I don't drive in Richmond anymore. She used to help me watch the signs, but I'm not quick enough in seeing the signs myself. You know how they change the streets—one week it's both ways and the next week it's one-way. When you get old, your reflexes get slow."

There is something in Miles Carpenter's speech that is not southern Virginia at all, and he's amused to be asked where he's *really* from.

"My family was from up near Lancaster. That's the Pennsylvania Dutch country. My mother and father both could speak the Dutch but I can't. I've lived here in this house since 1912, but people can still tell I'm from Pennsylvania. Funny, isn't it?"

Miles Carpenter has always worked with wood in one form or another. His father sold lumber in Pennsylvania, and when he moved to Virginia he opened a sawmill, located right over the ridge up behind the icehouse. The icehouse was built by Carpenter in 1915 and at that time he made his own ice.

"Now I have it shipped in from Petersburg," he explains. "I grow vegetables and watermelons and cantaloupes to sell, and so does my nephew. I sell his things too. In 1955 I retired from running the sawmill, and I just kept the icehouse going. It was after that when I went into carving *right*."

He's been doing wood carvings now for a long time, since he was only about fifty years old. "I started making things out of wood—animals and birds mostly—just to please my wife and I. I never thought anyone would

74

want to buy anything. I did this lady leading the greyhound and all those pigs and a lot of other small animals. One day I decided to make a big watermelon out of a tree trunk. You have to use an elm tree for a watermelon—that's the best kind—and it has to be a dead tree that died standing up. That way it's dried out, and it won't crack when you carve it. Elm isn't good to make other things at all. It's just good for watermelons. Anyhow, I carved this big watermelon—it must have weighed two hundred pounds—and then I painted it with house paint, good enamel paint with a nice shine to it. I painted it dark green and light green, just like a real watermelon, and every summer I would put it out in front of the stand to advertise what I was selling."

Carpenter becomes more and more animated as he reaches the important part of the story he's told so many times. "One day a fella passed by in a car, and what do you think he said? He said he'd like to buy it. That was in about 1970—I'd been using it in front of my stand for ten years or more. I told him I couldn't sell it, because I needed it to advertise my

watermelons, but I said I'd lend it to him in the winter. This fella, he was from the museum in Williamsburg—the Abby Aldrich Rockefeller Museum! So I loaned him the watermelon, and then when summer came he brought it back. The second year he came again and said he really wanted to buy it, so I figured I could carve another one. He said he'd give me one hundred and fifty dollars for it and—he was a very nice polite fella—he said, was that enough? I would have sold it for five dollars if someone had offered me that! So now it's in the museum, and I carved this one for my stand. I started to carve watermelon slices too, and to paint them red with the black seeds. I like to do them this way, with a bite out of them. Makes them look good to eat, don't you think?" He chuckles and pretends to take another bite from the wooden slice.

The range of Carpenter's fancy and inventiveness is constantly extending. He has made tall Indians, twenty-foot snakes, small chunky farm animals. He has carved marvelous creatures—real and imaginary— from twisted old roots. He has made mechanical figures that move their mouths and limbs when a string is pulled. Three boys with movable arms eat a watermelon. A red devil shovels a body into a pit. A blackbird pie opens to reveal twenty-six birds. Miles Carpenter is a man who likes to laugh, and his work has an engaging humor.

"I started making things out of roots because I seen something funny in them. I would look at roots from a tree that fell down, or I'd pull some up, and I'd look at all those long and short and thick and thin and tangled parts, and I'd just begin to see something funny. See, this one looks like it could be a bullfrog or an octopus or maybe . . ." He studies the root. "I think a bullfrog. Sometimes you get a big root and you can make a two-

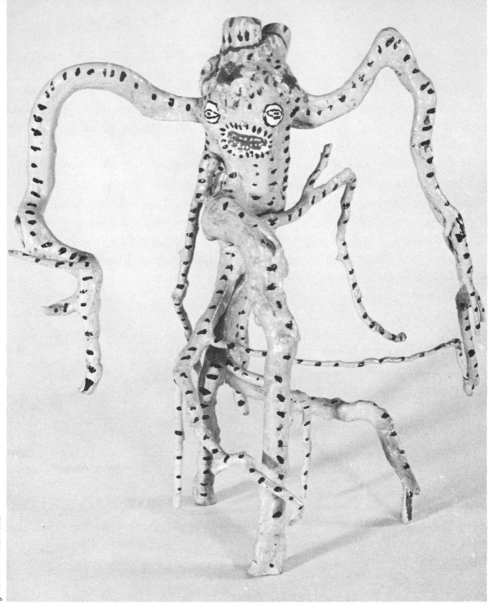

or three-headed monster like some of these. This octopus here—it was just a mess of roots. You have to be able to see something in a root—then you just fix it right."

His sculpting tools are a hatchet, a chisel, a coping saw, and a pocket-knife. By the door to the kitchen there is a large woodpile—the carver's supply of raw material. "I like to work mostly with poplar because it just works good. It's what you'd call a medium-soft wood. Then there's elm for watermelons. Everything I can't carve I use up in my old wood stove. This chunk here I've been looking at. I thought I'd make a lady's head that would be slim-like—a little out of the ordinary. I'd call her Venus."

He has great plans for the near and distant future. Tomorrow he's going to start work on the two roots a friend from Richmond found in the woods and brought to him. He has orders for more watermelon slices, and pretty soon he'll start on the Venus.

"I live alone, you know," he says. "When my wife passed away I was real despondent. I guess that's when I really took to carving more and more. It's a big help when you're real despondent to be able to do something like this." Carpenter sighs and then he smiles. "When you see my Venus she might make you laugh. Her arms will be kind of picked up, up over her head. Some might think her ugly, but if it's anything funny-lookin' or ugly-lookin'—that's what I really like best."

JOSHUA HORWITZ

Edward Ambrose

JOSHUA HORWITZ

He is a fine carpenter—not just an ordinary skilled workman but one of the best. He constructed a winding staircase without a single nail in it for the restoration of Sully Plantation. It's unlikely that anyone could design a job that he wouldn't be able to tackle with confidence and accomplish with distinction. Ed Ambrose is a man who has always been mechanically creative and quick with his hands, and—unlike most of the men and women in this book—what he really wanted to be from childhood onward was an artist.

"I mean a *real* artist," says the rangy Virginian, who has taught himself to carve and developed a style that's both rugged and distinctive. "When I got out of high school it was 1931 and it only cost twenty-five dollars to go to the Corcoran Art School in Washington, but in those years—it was depression, you know—I couldn't have begun to pay the room and board. So I went to work as a carpenter."

Ambrose lives, and has always lived, in the small town of Stephens City, just outside Winchester, Virginia. "My father was a cooper. He had forty Italian immigrants working for him making barrels. They used to pack lime in barrels in those days, and there's still plenty of limekilns out there in the valley."

The pleasant old white frame house on the main street of town in which Ambrose and his wife live has a front porch that has settled almost to pavement level. The house dates back to 1830, and everyone in Stephens City walks past it at least once every day. "Maybe it's older," Ambrose says. "I traced it back to 1830 for certain. It used to be a barbershop." Ambrose is interested in local history and he likes talking about his town. "Before the Civil War it was called New Town, and the population was a lot higher than it is now. The town had a newspaper and a funeral director and four doctors. There were tailor shops, and it was one of the biggest wagon-making towns in Virginia. In the 1940s there was an old man lived across the street—an old man in his eighties—and he told me that he was ten years old and he was settin' on that porch, that porch right across the street there, and he saw the damn Yankees come up the street heading for Winchester. I tell you, there's a lot of history in this little old place."

It's Sunday, and Ed Ambrose goes into the kitchen to stir his beans. His wife, who works in a bindery, is sunbathing in the backyard. "Mr. A. is a great chef," she calls out. "Don't forget to mention that. He does most of the cooking. His spareribs is delicious. He taught the scouts to cook blueberry pancakes and muffins. Tell about that, Mr. A."

Ambrose has been a scoutmaster for years. "I taught the boys how to cook and how to carve neckerchief rings. Things like that. I carved an Indian seven foot eleven inches tall for the scout building. Actually, it was eight feet tall, but it wouldn't fit in the building, so I had to cut off an inch."

He is not certain just when he started carving. "When I was a boy, about nine or ten, I'd take cigar boxes and make airplanes out of them. Later, when I got into carpentry, we'd stay at the job all week, and I'd just come home weekends. I always liked working on restorations—not on those high-rises. I worked on an old mill in Fairfax and then at Sully Plantation and out in the Manassas area. I was down in Norfolk a full year. I never knew anyone down where I was staying, and it suited me to sit out after supper with a piece of wood and a penknife. I'd sit up at night whittling and whittling. I always liked white pine best, and I'd just carve it out with a penknife and with what we call a utility knife. I never studied on it—I just did it. And I never stopped whittling, even when I dropped out of the union ten years ago so I could take jobs around here and stay home."

Ambrose says he's ready for social security next year but he plans to keep working. "There's a whole lot of restoration work around here now—you don't have to go live away from home to get work." He started selling his wood carvings after demonstrating carving at the Waterford fair fifteen years ago. Now he exhibits his work and demonstrates his technique right near home at Belle Grove Plantation's annual farm fair. He carves ducks,

cowboys, and old-time sea captains—and they're good sellers—but he takes most pride in his room settings. He is particularly pleased with the large general store and post office, his most ambitious work to date. It is still far from finished.

"This is a store from about 1890 or 1900," he explains. "On the counter there's a tobacco cutter—in the old days tobacco came in plugs and you cut it with one of these. This is a coffee grinder and that's a big cheese with a knife on the counter."

"The coffee mill works!" Mrs. Ambrose interjects. "Can you imagine anyone having the patience! He does, but I don't. Sometimes he asks me to help sand one of the pieces, but I tell him, 'Mr. A., I just don't have the patience like you do.'"

The store now has about 140 pieces of which eight are figures, standing about ten inches high. Two checker players sit rapt in concentration. A woman with a basket gives her order to the grocer. Two old men sit on a bench. One is peeling an apple, one whittling. Another man is busily carving a decoy. A cat perches on a sack of flour, watched by a dog. The name on the label on the flour sack is that of a local man who runs a mill.

There is a potbellied stove, a rack with axes. The shelves hold flatirons, pumpkins, bananas, hams, crockery, pitchers—each piece meticulously carved and painted, each piece historically justified.

"I'm going to add envelopes and newspapers for the cubbyholes in the post office racks, some rolls of sewing material, more hams, sugar, apples,

HN C. NEWCOMER (COLLECTION: JOAN PEARSON WATKINS)

kerosene, cracker barrels, boxes of oats—all the different things they sold in a good general store in those days."

There is also a blacksmith shop which is almost completed. "There's an old smith around here with a good name for his job, Atwood Rust. I'm going to make a sign for my blacksmith shop saying A. RUST, BLACKSMITH." Another of his room settings is a decoy shop, with shelves filled with small carved ducks.

One day he decided to do Richard Nixon hitchhiking on a highway with

83

a gas can in one hand. The carving was made in the fall of 1973, at the start of the gasoline crisis, when Nixon was president. "He's hot out there in the road," Ambrose explains, "so he's taken off his jacket. Did you ever see a picture of Nixon without his jacket?"

Ambrose sees a close relationship between building a house and making a carving. "When I build a house, I can see it in front of me all finished all the time I'm working on it—right from the start. Some people can't do this. When I'm working on a figure or a room setting, it's the same—I see it finished in front of my eyes."

As to why he has spent so many hours over the years with a block of wood in one hand and a penknife in another, the answer is easy: "Even now that I sell a good many things, I still can't get ten cents an hour on this, you know. People have no idea how long it takes, but that's not why I do it. It's just hard to explain how much pleasure—what a whole lot of pleasure—there is sitting out in the yard or here on the porch with a cold beer and workin' and thinkin' and workin' and thinkin'. I would have liked to have gone to art school and been a real artist, but I never did get to study on it nowhere, so I had to learn myself. It's a whole lot of pleasure— even if you're no real artist—in just being a whittler."

JOSHUA HORWITZ

CAROLYN JONES

Elijah Pierce

Elijah Pierce is eighty-three years old, and he can be found every day of the week at his barbershop in Columbus, Ohio, cutting hair or carving wood. "My customers won't let me quit," he says, and as if to prove the point, the customers keep arriving all through the day. When things are quiet the tall, thin barber sits down at his bench in a corner of the shop and picks up his tools.

Some of the men who come into the shop know that he has exhibited his wood carvings at the Columbus Gallery of Fine Art, at New York's Museum of Modern Art, at the Pennsylvania Academy of Fine Arts, at an international exhibition in Yugoslavia. Others just like the way he cuts their hair, and Elijah Pierce doesn't mind that one bit. In 1973, when the Columbus *Citizen-Journal* listed him as one of the city's ten most important men, Pierce accepted the compliment with his usual modesty. "I didn't even know I was an artist 'til they told me," he said. "I'll just keep on working same as I always have."

Pierce has been barbering, carving, and preaching the gospel for over half a century, but fame came to him late—in his seventy-ninth year. He was born in Mississippi in a log cabin, by the edge of a cotton field, the son of a former slave. His father was a religious man and a good farmer, and

Pierce says that the other eight children loved the farm. "All except me—I wanted to see the bright city lights," he says. "They called me the black sheep of the family." He left home with a nickel in his pocket, rode freight trains around the South, traveled to Ohio, married a woman from Danville, Illinois, and settled in Columbus. The day after his marriage he took a job in a barbershop, and some years later he acquired his own place, where he's been at work ever since.

When did the carving start? Pierce recalls that even as a boy he carved walking sticks, made figures from scraps of wood, carved pictures on tree trunks. One day in the 1920s he carved an elephant out of a small block of wood as a present for his wife's birthday. She liked it so much that she tied a ribbon around its neck and put it up on the living room mantel where it could be admired. He was enormously pleased by her response to the gift, and he began to carve a whole zoo of animals—every variety he could remember having seen in real life or in pictures. Soon he was carving whenever he had a break from his barbering. He began to carve reliefs in which biblical incidents were played out, often in an intricately designed series of scenes.

In the summertime Elijah Pierce and his wife would fill their car with his brightly painted wood carvings and travel around the state, visiting county fairs and church bazaars throughout the Midwest and the South. Pierce, who speaks of himself as a preacher, would talk about his carvings and expound on the biblical or moral lessons they demonstrated. The carvings were sold for small sums of money or given away, and the Pierces were pleased to simply make their travel expenses.

The powerful reliefs are painted in strong, glossy colors. Pierce uses enamel paints right from the can: "The kind you use for walls and woodwork," he says. "Nothing special about it." Often he obtains a glistening surface by sprinkling metallic "glitter" over his final wet coat of varnish.

The carvings are imaginative, original, and imbued with the artist's piety and sincerity. One, called *Vision of Heaven,* recalls a mystical experience in Pierce's childhood when his head was touched by the hand of God as he put down his Bible to read the Sears Roebuck catalogue. Pierce recalls that when the hand reached down he fell from his chair and was carried to his bed by his alarmed mother and sister, who thought he was dead. When he roused from his stuporous state, he recognized that God was displaying His power because of his disobedience.

Pierce has carved other incidents from his youth and scenes evoked by his father's recollections of slavery days. He has carved familiar scenes from the Bible—Noah's ark, Jonah and the fish, Jesus turning water to

wine, the garden of Gethsemane, Jesus baptized by John, the Nativity, the Crucifixion. He has lovingly carved a portrait of Martin Luther King. In his large piece titled *Pearl Harbor* one panel is devoted to the story of a queen in Africa who believed herself to be beautiful and was given a mirror

MICHAEL D. HALL (COLLECTION: MR. & MRS. MICHAEL D. HALL)

in which, for the first time, she saw herself as she really was. One powerful early carving is titled *Pilgrim's Progress*. The pilgrim pushes a heavy load of logs toward his savior, while men argue; women pose seductively; dice, cards, wealth, and whiskey lure the sinner.

Pierce, whose work now brings high prices from the most astute collectors, has no regret about his life of hard work and his years of obscurity. "I never went after any of these honors they've given me," he says. His work has been the intensely satisfying expression of a consuming religious devotion. "Every piece of work I got carved is a message, a sermon," he explains. "A preacher don't hardly get up in the pulpit without preaching some picture I got carved."

Mario Sanchez

Another carver of polychromed bas-reliefs is Mario Sanchez, a Floridian of Cuban descent. As a young man Sanchez was the brightest student who ever attended Professor Schultz's Commercial School in Key West. After receiving his certificate of qualification for secretarial work in both Spanish and English, he went to work as a bookkeeper. In his spare time Mario Sanchez began to make lively and colorful relief carvings of old Key West streets, buildings, festivities. In 1947 a folklore scholar and art gallery owner discovered his work, and his success has enabled him to devote himself to carving ever since.

The city he has recreated in his carvings is the Key West that he and his elderly mother remember in perfect detail. It is a world of old customs and of vanished landmarks—the old City Hall, the Fourth of July Café, the Gato Cigar Factory, the old waterworks, the demolished La Brisa amusement center, the vanished Caroline Lowe house. He remembers the signs painted on walls and on stores, the games children played in the streets, the shape of the old ice wagons, the festive air of the black burial processions. Like Clementine Hunter, Hattie Brunner, and Bruce Brice, Sanchez has a way of making a funeral look like a joyous occasion. There are, of course, the gorgeous flowers, and the band is playing, and everyone is all dressed up. It makes you want to get in step and follow the crowd.

89

Sanchez was born in Key West's Cuban neighborhood of Gato Village, where his father earned his living as a reader in a cigar factory. While the workers sorted tobacco and rolled cigars, Pedro Sanchez would stand on a platform and read aloud to them from Spanish newspapers and popular novels. The young Mario Sanchez shined shoes and attended St. Joseph's convent school and whittled scraps of driftwood he picked up on the beach. Later he used the well-cured boxes in which cigars were shipped from Cuba to Florida as boards for his first relief carving.

Although his carvings have been immensely popular, Sanchez shuns publicity and lives quietly, working at his lively and colorful Key West street scenes with a few simple chisels, a razor blade, a piece of broken glass. Most of his work has been created in the backyard of his mother's old house, under the shifting shadows of the banana and papaya trees. He draws a sketch on a large piece of brown paper, traces it onto a slab of cedar or cypress, and sets to work. When the carving is finished, he paints it with bright colors which he mixes with castor oil. "The smell brings back memories of childhood," he says with a smile.

Sanchez has always been interested in the history of his city, and he remembers that when the WPA sent writers to prepare a booklet on Key

West in the 1930s, he served as their guide and informant. Today he cannot produce enough carvings of his street scenes to meet the demand for his work, but his life has scarcely changed. He still smokes two-for-a-quarter cigars and works at a leisurely pace under the banana trees with his modest assortment of chisels and his dime store brushes. His reliefs hang in many distinguished collections and are permanently on display at Key West's El Kiosko Gallery. Cary Grant is an admirer and collector of his work, and he placed some Sanchez carvings on the walls of the set for the hotel scene in the film *That Touch of Mink*. The artist is unexcited, unflappable. He now lives in Tampa but he still spends time in Key West. He points to a carving and says simply, "That's the way it was when I was a boy." He scowls in newspaper pictures accompanying articles about a recent award, a one-man show. "If people don't like my stuff tomorrow I won't kill myself," he has said. "I can always shine shoes again and make a living."

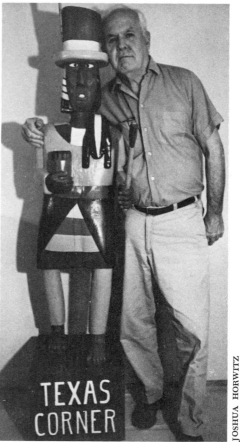

JOSHUA HORWITZ

Jim Colclough

Jim Colclough poses with an Indian he's carved for a restaurant, and then he walks over to a favorite piece. "Who's that?" he asks, and then he waits while you look. If you're slow he'll keep waiting—and prodding—until you guess. "Who's that? Of course he was younger then than in most of the pictures you've seen of him, but don't you recognize that face? Look at him."

It's Harry Truman, and Colclough carved a portrait of him for a very special reason. "I'm interested in genealogy and I had my family tree traced. That's a great thing, genealogy. They can tell you just about everything relating to your past. My ancestors came to this country in 1660, and one of my great-grandfathers ran pirates off the coast of Virginia. It's the truth—I'm not making any of this up. Another thing they turned up was the fact that old Harry Truman and I were related, and that's why I wanted to do a carving of him. We're not really close relatives, you understand.

JOSHUA HORWITZ

We're distant cousins. I wrote a letter to him when he was president, telling him that we were related, and I gave him the whole genealogy so he'd know all the other cousins too. I got a letter right back—not from Harry but from Bess. She said how glad they were to know all about that family tree and all about how we were cousins. It was a really nice letter."

When Colclough decided to begin his cousin's portrait, he considered a dignified presidential bust—very briefly. "What I decided was to make him looking like he did when he was an artillery captain in World War I. It took me all one day to lace up those boots." The carving is redwood and the boots are laced with copper wire. Colclough's expression becomes mischievous. "Let me show you something kind of special about Harry," he says, with a half-suppressed grin. He pulls the crank at the base of the statue, and Harry Truman lifts his arm and thumbs his nose at the world. "That's old Harry, all right," says Colclough, overcome with delight at the visitors' surprise.

Truman is not the only distinguished relative in Colclough's genealogy. There is also the Duchess of Windsor, carved standing beside the Duke.

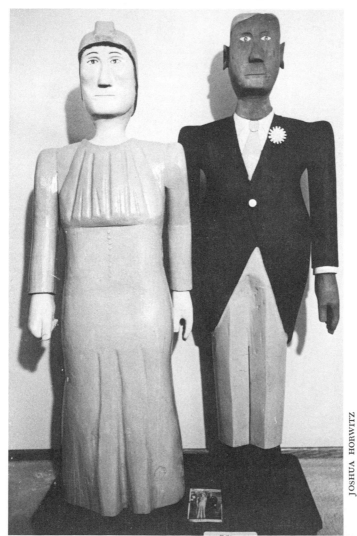

The elegantly dressed couple stare out at the world with expressions of bored solemnity. "They're at their wedding," Colclough explains. Having seen Truman's tricks the visitor suddenly fears that the Duke and Duchess may begin jogging or go into a wrestling match, but they simply stand there waiting for something to happen, quite glum.

It now seems to Jim Colclough that he always wanted to carve, and he can't quite figure out why he didn't start earlier, but he took up the art only ten years ago, after the death of his wife. His early pieces were inspired by his career as a carnival barker. "I sure saw some things I wanted to carve then," he says. Born in Fort Smith, Arkansas, he worked first as a car salesman but lost his job during the depression. He joined the carnival and traveled with the show for thirty years, and when he began to carve, his mind was filled with memories of the three-breasted woman, the half-man–half-woman, the two-headed boy, the minotaur. Some of his work is packed away in another house, some was sold, some given away. Colclough is not interested in selling his favorites, the carvings that relate most closely to his life.

"Look here at this guy. Ever seen anyone doing this job? See what he's doing? Look at him. You tell me what he's doing." What he's doing is shoveling out an outhouse. He is a chunky man in a helmet with a grave expression on his stolid face. His tiny donkey waits patiently to draw the

cart away. Turn the crank and the man goes to work. The shovel moves back and forth from the outhouse to the cart. "How's that?" says Colclough, roaring with self-appreciation and holding his nose. "Bet you never saw anything like that!"

The carvings are all made from California redwood, large pieces of driftwood found along the beaches near the town of Westport, where Colclough now lives. At the age of seventy-four he is a tall and powerful-looking man with handsome white hair and a taste for a good joke. Some of the carvings, like the Windsors and his life-sized Indian, are painted. Others, like Harry Truman, are finished with linseed oil. A great number are mechanical or humorous or grotesque or all three. Often it's difficult

to understand the joke unless you know the details of Colclough's biography.

"Me and my wife built our dream house some years ago. It was down there where that fellow Hearst built *his* dream house. Ever been to San Simeon? Well, we built our wonderful dream house, and the next thing, they decided to put a freeway through there. They took my land and they gave me next to nothing. That's what this carving is all about. You see this—that's the government of California—that demon kind of creature. He's got hold of this guy and if you turn the crank he'll give him a good shaking down. I call that piece 'Helping Man Decide Sell Home for Highway.' How do you like that title? That's how he convinces him, you see? A good carving has to be something about your life."

Colclough turns the piece so that his signature shows. "When I told a friend about my distinguished genealogy, she said I should really sign my name 'Sir,' but I told her I'm a Southerner in ancestry and in the South they say 'Suh.' So since then I've been signing all my work that way— 'Suh Jim Colclough.' "

The ideas pour forth, inspired by a full and varied experience. "There's another piece I did that you'd like, of a drunk hanging off a horse. That was a while back . . . and the donkey carving over at the other house has a recording hooked up to it and a poem written by a friend that's on one side . . . and I wish I could show you the half-man–half-woman. I call it 'Half and Half Pipe Mixture.' I tried to sell it to the Half and Half people, but they wouldn't buy. It's a big one, life-sized, divided down the middle, not crossways like you usually see them. There's lots of things to carve if you look back a lot and have a good memory."

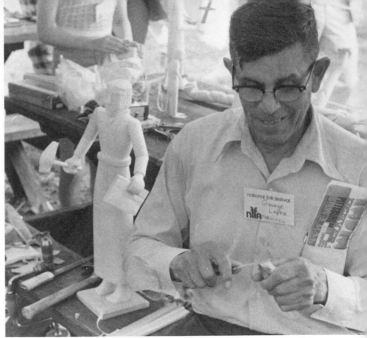

George Lopez

JOSHUA HORW

Another folk carver from the western part of the United States is George Lopez of Cordova, New Mexico, shown here demonstrating his skill at a 1974 crafts fair at Wolf Trap Farm in Fairfax, Virginia. He is a descendant of early Spanish settlers in the area, and his life and thought have been molded by the old Spanish culture into which he was born. He lives in the town where his father and grandfather lived and died, and he says that he is a sixth-generation carver. At seventy-five, George Lopez is the patriarch of a family in which three sons, a daughter, grandsons, a daughter-in-law, and a niece all carve. Members of the family who have no artistic ability help out as sanders.

George Lopez is often referred to as a *santos* carver—a term used in New Mexico to denote someone who makes representations, either painted or carved in the round, of saints and biblical figures. The fact that he and other members of the family carve small animals, trees, and other secular designs in addition to the figures of Catholic iconography distinguishes these contemporary New Mexican carvers from the *santeros* of old, but the designation is still commonly used.

Lopez, who will speak only Spanish with new acquaintances, is assisted by his nineteen-year-old grandson and apprentice, Alex Lopez Ortiz, who travels with him and acts as translator. The word *santo,* he explains, means "blessed." Therefore, a *santo* is any object that has been officially blessed.

"Anything blessed by the priest becomes a *santo,* and then it cannot be sold," he says. "A carving should be taken by the owner to be blessed after it's bought, and then it will have the same holy power. Anything can become *santo*. Your new car can become *santo*—and then you will drive in safety, protected from the witches who lure cars off the road."

The old saint carvings which were made in New Mexico from the early Spanish colonial period onward were the native religious folk art of the region. The *santero* was a man of artistic talent who taught himself to carve and then went about in a cart pulled by a burro, traveling from village to village, peddling his wares and accepting commissions for a holy painting (*retablo*) or a carving (*bulto*) of a favorite saint to be set in a household niche and revered. The *santero* was the New Mexican equivalent of the itinerant portrait painter of New England. Each man developed his own style of work and his own geographical territory. Traditionally, *santeros* did not sign their creations. Few of the old *santeros* are identified today, although early *bultos* and *retablos* are now avidly collected by individuals and by museums.

George Lopez's father, José Dolores Lopez, was a weaver, carpenter, goatherd, and repairer of the *bultos* in the village. Although he was the son of a *santero*, he himself did not take up carving until middle age, after the death of his father. He began to carve at a time when his concern for his oldest son—who had been taken into the army in World War I and sent to France—made him wakeful and restless at night. What started as an insomnia cure became a passion. The son, Nicudemos, returned home in perfect health, but the father seized every moment he could from his farm work to carve his saints. "No one showed me the cuts," he often told villagers. "It was God who put the idea into my head."

A friend from outside the Spanish community suggested to José Lopez that there was a market for secular carvings, and the skilled worker then began producing wooden toys, carved hanging shelves, small figures of animals. He died in 1937 after an auto accident. Some years later, his three sons began carving in earnest. George Lopez, who is the second son, has worked as a shepherd in northern New Mexico and as a laborer in Los Alamos. He did some figures in the early forties, but he began carving full time in 1952, when he returned permanently to Cordova from Los Alamos. His materials are cottonwood, cedar, and white pine. His work has been given considerable recognition, and in 1971 he was awarded an honorary degree at the University of Colorado.

The members of the Lopez family refer to their saints' images simply as carvings, not as *santos*. They are frequently sold to people who are more interested in their aesthetic charm than in their possible usefulness as an aid to prayer or a symbol of devotion.

George's tall figure of San Miguel is a traditional subject, which he has

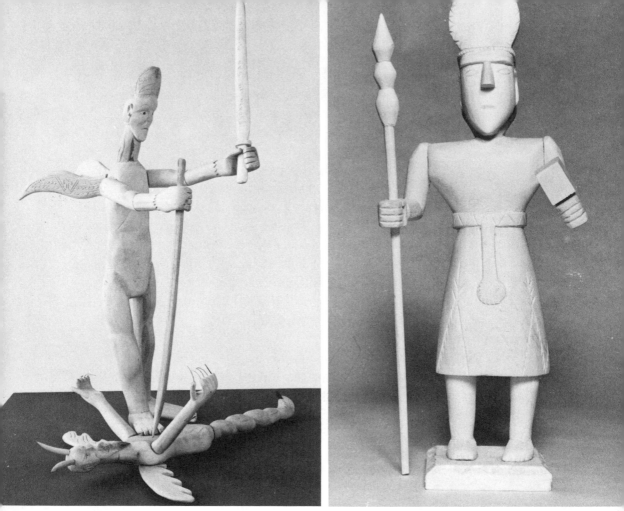

C. MICHAEL DEPUNTE
(COLLECTION: HERBERT W. HEMPHILL, JR.)

JOSHUA HORWITZ
(COLLECTION: MR. & MRS. J. RODERICK MOOR

carved frequently, usually on a smaller scale. The story is of St. Michael, the archangel who overcame Lucifer, the leader of the heavenly angels in revolt. When Lucifer was thrown from heaven, his beautiful angelic face and form were miraculously altered into the inhuman appearance of a demon. San Miguel stands triumphant in a Roman posture of victory, with his sword held high and his foot planted on his victim. King Herod is another favorite subject. The little figure stands in a rigid frontal posture looking strangely Egyptian. In an elaborate many-piece carving, Adam and Eve—a perennially favorite subject among folk artists—stand beside the tree of life, in which a horned Satan lurks.

Lopez is always anxious that the meaning of *santo* be understood by outsiders. He points to a carving of a saint. "This is not a *santo*, it is just *palos*— just a block of wood—unless it is blessed," he explains. "It is like you, if you have not been baptized. What are you if the priest has not blessed you? You are nothing but a stick of wood."

100

Total Environmentalists

Joseph Bell

"I never had education," Joseph Bell explains. "I was in the first grade for about six years and the teacher told my mother that I shouldn't be in school—I was too nervous. They said I would learn just as much at home."

Joseph Bell, aged fifty-five, is a lonely man, deeply grieved by the recent death of his mother, with whom he lived all his life. He has worked intermittently at solitary jobs—as a night watchman, as a janitor. He does not read or write. He never married. He lives in Staunton, Virginia, on the highway that leads to Buffalo Gap. He has built many extraordinarily inventive and beautiful wind machines. At one time the small house in which

he and his mother lived was surrounded by thirty to forty of his creations, ranging in length from four to twelve feet, each bearing twenty or more propellers.

Bell's sister, who has come to stay with him, points with pride to a workmanlike corner cabinet, a hanging bookshelf, a glass-fronted cupboard —all pieces her brother made. "He's always been so good at these things," she says. "He should have had more encouragement to go out on his own, to be independent."

Raised high on a thirty-foot length of pipe, behind the house where Joseph Bell still lives, one of his triumphs whirls and revolves in the wind. The rest have been sold. It is made of wood scraps and sheet metal painted with large dots of green, red, white, and yellow. The four large discs revolve and the tail spins round and round. Despite its size—it is about

JOSHUA HORWITZ

twelve feet long—the simplicity of the design makes this one of his less ambitious pieces.

"I call them windmills," Bell says, "but a fellow who bought one calls them whirligigs!" He laughs at the amusing traditional term, repeating the word over and over.

Joe Bell doesn't know quite how he conceived the idea of making his first pinwheel-windmill-whirligig. "I was fooling around with tin can lids," he recalls, "and I wanted to see what I could do, so I stuck some into a piece of wood and put a hole in the middle and took it out in the wind, and it started spinning up a storm." He had always enjoyed watching airplanes as a child and, in adulthood, he became interested in making model planes. He says he would have liked to be in the Navy Air Force. It was perhaps a decade ago that he moved on to constructing increasingly intricate and fanciful whirligigs, and within a few years the entire yard became a riot of revolving propellers. When he exhibited a few at a crafts show, they sold immediately, and he made some more.

The wind machines are made from discarded materials—used scraps of wood and metal. His "spinners," with blades cut from venetian blind slats or tin can lids, are inserted into blocks of wood and bent and alternated in such a fashion that they catch the wind from different directions. "One windmill had thirty-eight spinners on its tail," he says. "Another one is a big airplane with a gunner inside. It's the tail that guides them. That's how they go around—by the tail."

The whirligigs have been displayed at Mary Baldwin College and have been snapped up by collectors and dealers. Joe Bell isn't sure he's going to make any more. He is deeply depressed by the loss of his mother, and he

106

views the future with uncertainty. But the sight of the windmills glittering in the sunlight and whirling in the wind cheers him considerably. "I haven't had a bit of education," he says, spinning a small propeller on a stick. "My brothers have education, but they don't know anything about how to make a windmill!"

JOSHUA HORWITZ

Dow Pugh

Although he lives alone in a cabin crammed with the extraordinary clutter of objects he has made, bought, picked up here and there, Dow Pugh has a business card. It reads: "Loranzo Dow Pugh, retired; Indian, Snake and Gourd Man; Monterey, Tenn." In the four corners of the card are the words: "No money," "No phone," "No address," "No business."

107

"I never been called anything but 'Dow,' " he explains, "but Loranzo is my real first name. I think my folks named me after a drummer they knew. I looked and looked up in the family cemetery up in Crab Tree, Tennessee, to see if there was ever a Loranzo in the family, and they got darn near ever' name you ever heard of—but no Loranzo."

Pugh was born in eastern Tennessee. He worked for many years as a machinist in Battle Creek, Michigan, but in 1958 he came back home. "My son got killed on a bicycle, my wife died, so I just live here alone, and I have to keep busy. I'm no artist," he insists, motioning toward his wood carvings, rock sculptures, tall concrete figures, paintings, gourd carvings, life-sized Indians, "just got to keep busy like my mother. She's over ninety, and she's been working on a fancy quilt all summer—just can't sit still and do nothin'."

This restlessness hardly begins to explain the exterior and interior environment Pugh has created up behind the split rail fence surrounding his place. Outside the house are wall paintings, sculptures, Indian artifacts. The rear of the house and two worksheds are covered with designs, flowers, Indian writing, the faces of characters familiar from history or from animated cartoons or the comics. Lincoln and Washington share wall space with Mighty Mouse and Alley Oop. Two almost life-sized figures made of painted concrete guard the house, looking a bit ferocious. One is a cowboy, the other a spaceman. The spaceman's mouth is peculiarly distorted. "I was

going to put a cigar up in the corner of his mouth—a big fat one. I made it and painted it, but when I went to put it in, the cement had dried and the space had closed." The glassy-looking eyes are made with the balls from roll-on deodorant bottles. "They make the best eyes of all," Pugh says, revealing one of his secrets.

Two life-sized sunbathers molded in concrete lie on a rock taking the sun with a lizard, a snake, and a turtle. There are rocks painted to resemble animals; a comic face is painted on a flint ball; two bathers, a man and a woman, are portrayed life-sized on the workshop doors. "That's me," says Pugh, standing by the figure of the man. "That's me before I growed my mustache."

Dow Pugh is a knowledgeable and enthusiastic hunter of Indian remains, and his land is in the center of an area that was a Cherokee reservation until 1813. He has found literally thousands of arrowheads, nut-cracking stones, tomahawks, stone tools, and other artifacts in the woods near his house. His collections are kept outdoors and indoors and in the homes of his brothers and friends.

The interior of Dow's house is a dizzying and dazzling sight. It's impossible to know what to look at first. The main room of the cabin has three pieces of furniture: an old bed, a ruptured chair, and a television set. The rest of the decor is a fascinating conglomeration of objects he's made and collected: Civil War hats, World War I helmets, old golf caps, plaster life masks, tomahawks, gourds made into baskets and faces, carved heads, carved masks, mounted stuffed fish, snake skins, a skull with Ping-Pong balls in the eye sockets, old musical instruments, Appalachian scooped bowls carved out of buckeye. There are also paintings. An Indian head wears a reddish wig. "I bought it to wear myself," says Pugh, "but it was too hot, so I give it to him." There are a few skeletons tucked away here and there in boxes.

Pugh is busy with plans for more and more figures—he'll carve two life-sized Indians this winter as he sits by his fire. The fireplace was part of the cabin in which his parents and grandparents were born, but the cabin itself burned down long ago. "My grandpa was twelve years old when one of those damn Yankees made him dance in front of this fireplace," he says. "His father had made him a coonskin hat, and he'd gone to sleep in it like kids do, you know, and that night the Yankees made a raid and came into the cabin. One of them took his coonskin hat and pushed an old felt hat on his head instead and made him dance. My grandpa never forgot it.

It made him so mad. On his deathbed he said he was gonna get that man who took his coonskin hat and made him dance. He never forgot it."

Pugh shows more of his treasures: the wing of a twenty-pound turkey his brother shot, a big stuffed bass a cousin caught in Florida, an old bear trap, four huge "bushel" gourds, a ukulele with the body made from a ham tin, the skull of a squaw, a snake in a jar of preservative.

He is planning more pieces of concrete sculpture, inspired by a recent success. "A man around here lost his dog, and he thought a whole lot of that dog. He asked me to make a figure of him for a monument. Well, I made it out of concrete and out back I picked some of those little seeds on the bush—the ones they call mole beans. I used them for the ticks—stuck them in the cement when it was damp. I tell you, that man was well pleased with the effect."

The Indian, Snake, and Gourd Man sets out seed and scraps for the birds, squirrels and racoons. He explains his plans for a new mechanism for the well. He is carving a chair and plans to make a large gourd into a sewing basket. There is always so much to do. The paint is flaking off one of the sheds, and it will have to be scraped and then repainted with new faces and new designs.

An interest in portraiture has resulted in the head of a youthful Hitler carved in buckeye. Theodore Roosevelt, rendered in house paint on card-

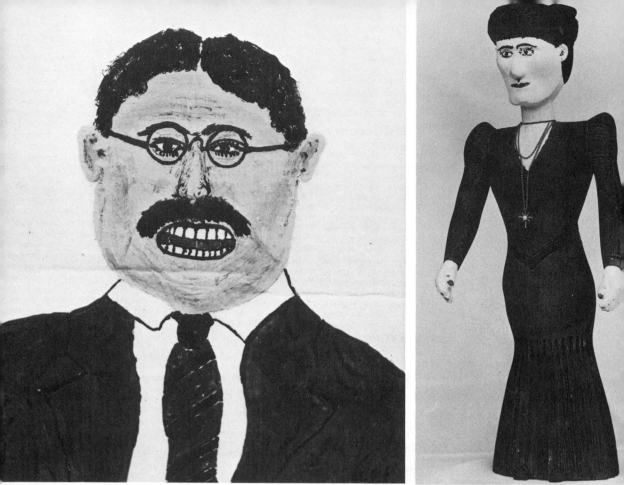

board, grins heartily. Pugh feels that the Rough Rider's eyes are too close together, but readily admits that the spirit of the man comes through.

He modestly accepts compliments on the fine figure of an "old-fashioned woman" carved in buckeye and brightly painted. "I just can't sit down without something to whittle on," he protests, laughingly. "I'm what you call a jack-of-all-trades and good for nothing."

Walter Flax

JOSHUA HORWITZ

Yorktown, Virginia, plays host to sightseers all year around. It is a fine place to go in conjunction with a visit to Jamestown and Colonial Williamsburg. You can take a self-guided battlefield tour after watching a dramatic film about the 1781 defeat of the British forces under General Cornwallis. You can view the impressive and strategically located harbor and visit George Washington's headquarters, the old Grace Church, any number of gravestones and monuments, and nine distinguished eighteenth-century buildings.

If, however, you became totally lost on the way to Yorktown and pulled onto the shoulder of the highway some miles down from the Visitor's Center, you might notice a path heading away from the road and into the woods. If you climbed over the low cable barrier and hiked up the path and took a left by the large clump of huckleberry bushes and made the correct turn each time the path forked, you would come to a clearing in the woods where you could no longer hear the sound of cars heading toward the battlefield. You would find yourself smack in the middle of the fantasy world created by Walter Flax.

Walter Flax is a flamboyantly eccentric man, the commander of an extraordinary fleet of battleships. Although Yorktown natives have seen Flax riding about on his bicycle for decades, no one seems to know very much about this solitary man who lives in the woods, wears an old gob hat in summer and a tattered World War I uniform in winter, has a devastatingly charming smile, and loves cigars. Very few of the people who have hired him over the years to do odd jobs know that his home is an unimproved two-room frame cabin surrounded by hundreds of ship models, all

113

of which he has constructed over the years from scraps of wood and metal and assorted junk and found objects.

To Flax they are "somethin'-like ships. Some is somethin'-like battleships and some is cruisers and some gunships." There is a tugboat and a submarine and, over by the side of the cabin, two airplanes.

Flax has enjoyed a lifetime infatuation with oceangoing vessels, although the only occasion on which he boarded a ship was when he rode the steamer that used to run from Norfolk to Baltimore. When he was younger he spent much of his time looking at submarines, battleships, and tankers at the shipyard in Newport News, the Yorktown Naval Weapons Station, the Portsmouth Naval Yard in Norfolk, the nearby Amoco refinery. Not long ago he rode his bicycle twenty-seven miles to look at some ships, but he says that, these days, "I mostly get my types from magazine pictures."

The fleet is a fascinating display of ingenuity in the use of cast-off materials; its condition is a study in all the stages of decay of metal and wood. Starting, in most cases, with partially rotted wood and rusted metal, Flax never made any attempt until very recently to preserve his creations. As they disintegrate, he cannibalizes them to make new models. In recent months he has started covering some of the ships with gray paint. "It keeps 'em fresher," he says, with an enormous grin.

Walter Flax is a lifelong scavenger who never overlooks a throwaway piece of metal he can carry home on his handcart. "I go down to that Fort Eustis, that artillery camp. The government, they sure throw away a lot of stuff you can use. They sure does." The stuff is now part of the great mothball fleet. A careful look reveals that what, at first glance, looks like actual nautical hardware is a conglomeration of old telephone dials, toasters, a rusted clock, a toy cash register, a lampshade frame. There are balls and light bulbs, a stereopticon viewer, the drainer from a sink, the regulator from a kerosine stove, a soap holder, old cans, ashtrays of every sort.

"I get the pieces and I find where the solidness comes and I piece 'em up. I'm gettin' too old to keep them boats up right," he says cheerfully.

Flax's dream world includes a vision of his fleet sailing in the water. The boats measure from about two feet in length to twenty or twenty-five feet.

JOSHUA HORWITZ

He keeps an old icebox which lies on its side filled with water. "That's a pond to sail 'em in, but it's too small," he says matter-of-factly.

Although he appears to be in his early seventies, the artist is not sure of his age. He says that he was raised by his grandmother, and seems to have lived alone since he was a teenager. He neither reads nor writes, and he occasionally calls himself by other names. He has difficulty sorting out his memories, but says at times that he would have liked to be in the navy. "When that first war came, I wasn't smart enough," he explains, with no evidence of remorse. "When that second war came, I was too game-legged."

If you ask him why he has spent virtually all his adult life in this secluded clearing constructing make-believe ships, he seems surprised. "I don't know —it just got into me."

Was it the Yorktown aura of former naval glory? Did he start with the idea of making just one ship, or had he planned on a fleet from the start? Why did he do it? When pressed for further explanations, he talks for a while about Hitler, about Newport News, about cigars and his bicycle—

and then he laughs. "I'm gifted thataway. Sometimes you got something you can do—other people *can't* do it." He cocks his cigar in the corner of his mouth and surveys—with total satisfaction—his enormous and glorious fleet.

SHUA HORWITZ

Creek
Charlie

He was a gentle and soft-hearted man who loved children, although he never had any of his own. He never left home and he never married. He was one of eleven offspring of Bill and Dellie Warrick Fields, and his brothers and sisters always knew that it was he who would take care of Momma. When the brothers and sisters grew up and married and went off to work in the nearby fields and coal mines, Charlie stayed with his widowed mother in the small four-room frame house beside Cedar Creek. Several of the boys left the mountains to go into the army in the First World War, but he was exempt because of his filial responsibility. He grew fifteen acres of tobacco and he always had a vegetable garden. When he was young he also raised turkeys. It is estimated that his annual income may have come to as much as one thousand dollars. He never learned to read or write, but he always enjoyed looking at the pictures in magazines.

When his mother died, Charlie Fields was forty-five or perhaps fifty years old. Soon afterward he began painting the house, and he continued to work on it until his death. In his old age he became very fond of bees. He kept thirty-eight hives, but he rarely took the honey, because—as he told everyone who asked—the bees worked so hard to make it that it just didn't seem right. In accordance with the predictions of local folklore, when Charlie Fields died, on December 21, 1966, at the age of eighty-three, his bees left the hives, flew away, and never returned.

He is survived by an octogenarian brother named Rob and remembered by many people in the nearby town of Lebanon, in the southwest corner of the state of Virginia. One old miner says that three days before his death, Charlie, who had not been a churchgoer, had himself baptized down at the creek. "He died happy," the friend says insistently.

No one knows why he painted the house like he did, but Creek Charlie was a good man, they tell you. A few people worried about their children going to visit, because sometimes you can't tell about old men who live alone, but there was never a problem, not a single whisper. It may look like a kind of peculiar business to an outsider, they tell you, but no one's going to say anything bad about Charlie Fields, because he's dead now and he never hurt anyone in his whole life. He loved his mother and took good care of her until she died. After that he just stayed home and painted polka dots on the house. Nothing wrong with that.

The house has been empty since his death. To go there you drive a few miles out of Lebanon and then turn onto a dirt road. Just about the time when you suddenly hear the loud rushing of the creek, you will see the house sparkling red, white, and blue against the green hillside. You must leave your car on the road and walk across the broad creek on the foot-bridge, one person at a time, and watch how you step. Charlie built it to replace the old swinging bridge his daddy had put up, but that was maybe thirty or forty years ago. Now the "new" bridge is decaying, and you have

MICHAEL SMITH

to take care, or you could go right through a rotted board. From the bridge a path leads to the house.

When he died, Charlie left the house to his brother. Rob lives over the mountain in the village of Cleveland and can't get by often to see to things. The other brothers and sisters have all died. "I'se the baby," says Rob, laughing at the joke and coughing on his tobacco juice. In September the papaws ripen by Charlie's house, and Rob goes over to gather the fruit when it falls from the trees. It troubles him to see the weeds growing up to the windowsills, and the wonderful Ferris wheel out over the gate fallen into ruins, and the mess in the front room. The house was ransacked by vandals five years ago, but what can Rob do? He means to find a boy to cut the grass, it looks so bad. It just doesn't seem right. Charlie always kept the place so perfect, everything so fresh and tidy.

The house, which Charlie's father built when the children were young, is painted—inside and out—with polka-dotted designs. Each board is painted, the tin roof is painted, the window frames are painted, and so is the chimney. Inside, the walls, floors, ceilings, doors are completely covered with striking—sometimes intricate—patterns. The colors are ordinary house paint. Because friends brought him their leftovers, a few

sections of the house have touches of brown and green, but the color scheme is almost entirely red, white and blue. "Charlie, he sure liked Uncle Sam," says Rob, with a shrill cackle. A vivid American flag is painted on the upper part of the front door. To the left of the door, the mounted head of a deer—a gift from an old friend—hangs weather-beaten and decayed, staring with ruined eyes at the haunting remains of the front yard playground.

Rob sits and chews tobacco on his front porch and reminisces about the time—so long ago—when Charlie started his painting. "Well, you know, it had to be after Momma died. She wouldn't *never* have let him do it." He makes a gesture of astonishment. "To tell the truth, I didn't know what to think when he started in. None of us did. We thought he might be losin' his mind. First he started a-dottin' and a-dottin' the outside, and then he started a-dottin' and a-dottin' the inside! You know what he did then? He started a-dottin' the furniture. Even the clocks!" Rob shakes his head with the wonder of it all. "Momma wouldn't never have let him do *that!*"

As the years went on, Charlie Fields fell completely under the grip of his remarkable compulsion. He painted his bright stripes and squiggles and wavy lines and squares filled with crosses and bull's-eyes and, most of all, polka dots on everything he owned. He built beehives in the form of small models of his own house, and he painted them with red, white, and blue polka-dotted designs. Six of the hives were built inside the house, with passages through the wall to the exterior. Glass panels allowed him to view the bees at their work. On the front and side porches he used soft-drink bottles as horizontal members between narrow wooden railings,

and he painted them white with red dots, or sometimes red with white dots. His bedroom has a brilliant red, white, and blue floor, painted in concentric circles. The walls are striped with red and dotted, and the ceilings have a fresh bold red and white pattern. The stovepipe is dotted; the chairs are dotted; the tables are dotted.

The house has been stripped of many of its furnishings. At one time it was filled with model airplanes, which were suspended from the ceiling. Only one remains. Charlie fashioned an arbor of painted pipe and large-sized grapefruit juice cans to decorate the front room. He twined paper roses around it, and a few still hang there limply. He made collages with pictures he clipped from magazines and calendars. His favorite subjects were mothers with children and Franklin D. Roosevelt. He picked up hundreds of old dolls and discarded toy soldiers and cheap ceramic animals, and he painted them with polka dots and set them around the rooms.

Some people around Lebanon say that he talked to the dolls.

A strange painted wood carving of a minstrel show used to stand in the front room. The small figures jiggle up and down on wires, and two old paper dolls and one small tin doll have been incorporated into the group.

When Rob left the mines and went to work as a prison guard, he brought Charlie a carving of the Crucifixion made by one of the prisoners. Charlie liked it. He put it up on the mantel, painted it with polka dots, and wired it with Christmas tree lights. Then he wired the exterior of the house with more little colored lights, and he built model airplanes, a carousel, a Ferris wheel, and some mechanical wind-driven toys to decorate the front yard. He lined the path with old tires, standing them on end, and he

painted them red and white. Today the tires extend to the gate; at one time they went all the way to the bridge.

"When he got older I'd go up to the house every week and bring Charlie groceries," Rob says, "because he didn't have nothing to eat except what he growed and the carp he fished out of the creek. Momma kept two good milk cows but when she died he sold them. I used to tell Charlie things would be a lot easier for him if he got married and had someone to cook his supper. He had a girlfriend for about twenty years, but then she got to knowing he wasn't a marrying sort and she married another fella. Charlie used to tell me he'd make like he was married to see how it felt. He'd set two plates at the table and he'd make his biscuits and put one on each plate. Then he'd put some greens on each plate. First he'd eat his greens and biscuits and then he'd eat hers. He'd laugh and he'd say, 'You know, if I really had a wife she'd eat it up herself and I'd only have but one biscuit.'

"After Charlie got the house all painted, he had a girl in town to write him a sign saying 'Come on in. You're welcome in here,' and he put the sign by the door. Sunday was the day for visiting. He never kep' a lock on the door, and people came—I tell you—people came from all over. Charlie would wear his polka-dot suit and greet the guests down by the gate or at the spring. I can't even tell you what that suit was like. It was a regular shirt and pants and shoes and a hat, and then he took his brush and painted them all over with polka dots.

"Charlie had the guests to sign a big book he had and there must have been thousands of names. It was thirty or forty years, you know, that people came a-visitin'. He painted the house over and over, so it was sometimes different from now, and he built new things. He let the children play with everything, turn the Ferris wheel and the merry-go-round and pick up all the toys. There was about twenty dolls a-settin' on that merry-go-round and dolls and toys on the Ferris wheel and in the airplanes. When a mother smacked a child for touching things, he'd say, 'You smack on me when you do that.' He loved children, Charlie did. He loved for people to come to his house. He said there was no place like his house in the whole world."

The Sunday suit still hangs in the bedroom. No one knows quite what to do with it. Some people remember that at one time in the past the outside of the house was striped, and at another period the design was an allover checkerboard pattern. But Charlie kept returning to polka dots. A young man from Lebanon says his father told him he went by one day and saw Charlie painting big dots with his fingers—just dipping them in the bucket

124

—but Rob is shocked by the idea and fastidiously insists Charlie always used a brush.

In 1960 a newspaper reporter from Bristol, Tennessee, interviewed Creek Charlie and wrote a story about the house. When he asked the remarkable artist why he had created this fantastic fairy-tale environment, Charlie said he just didn't know, he thought maybe he'd done it "to make the youngsters laugh."

Rob reports that Charlie left home on only one occasion. Two boys from

125

the local area had to be escorted to a prison farm near Richmond, and Charlie took the job. "He went all the way to Richmond on the Greyhound, and I tell you, he liked that trip. When he come back he said the boys was no trouble and the people in Richmond, they fed him real good. But he never left home before that, and he never left after that, not ever again."

Until his death Charlie Fields stayed down by the noisy creek painting and repainting the little house with total absorption, patience, and devotion. There is something intensely moving about the sight of the deserted structure on which decades of loving attention were lavished. If Creek Charlie was lonely six days a week, there is no question about the fact that on Sundays he was a happy and expansive host who responded with delight to the wonder and admiration of his guests. Each Sunday he would don the polka-dotted suit, straighten the dolls, hoist the airplanes, give the Ferris wheel a twirl, and walk toward the bridge to greet the first visitors of the day. No one has reported that his ghost still walks along the bottomland down by the creek, but it is impossible not to feel his presence. On a Sunday morning, when the sun hits the red, white, and blue paint on the front of the house and the wind jogs the propeller of the remaining front yard airplane and the shattered Ferris wheel gives a plaintive screech, you can stand by the bridge and squint your eyes in just the right way, and— if you have a mind to—you can see Creek Charlie coming down the path to shake your hand.

James Hampton

A paper tacked to a bulletin board bore the injunction from Proverbs 29:18, "Where there is no vision the people perish." Along the entire wall ranged an elaborate many-part construction of wood and cardboard and pieces of old furniture—completely surfaced with silver and gold foil. Astonishingly, the shabby, inconspicuous garage contained a dazzling homemade rendition—fashioned entirely from cast-off materials—of the interior appointments of a church or cathedral, complete with thrones, altars, pulpits, standards, offertory tables, icons, crowns, and other ecclesiastical embellishments.

James Hampton's creation, officially titled *The Throne of the Third Heaven of the Nations Millenium General Assembly,* was discovered after his death. It is now owned by the Smithsonian Institution in Washington, D.C., located a short distance from the garage on Seventh Street, N.W., where it was built. No one knows why Hampton was inspired to give every minute of his spare time, year after year, to the construction of this bizarre and unique masterpiece. And yet every detail of the Throne speaks of the ecstatic devotion of its creator.

127

In December 1964, the wide doors of the garage were thrown open for the first time and the sun shone in on the glittering surfaces of the Throne of the Third Heaven. Hampton, who earned his living as a laborer employed by the federal government, had rented the garage for fourteen years from a man named Meyer Wertlieb, who owned a clothing store half a block away. Each month the rent was delivered promptly and in person, and Wertlieb never questioned Hampton closely about why a poor man who owned no car would want to pay fifty dollars a month for a large garage.

"He told me he had things to store and that he was working on something and it might come to something some day. I thought he fixed furniture there, because in the summer I'd walk through the alley and I'd stop to kibitz with him. There was a big door to the garage that could open wide enough to get a truck in, and then there was a little door for a man to go in and out. Hampton was always sitting out in the alley by the little door, fiddling with something. He'd have a chair or a table and some nails and glue, and he always had tinfoil. Sometimes I'd see winos come bring him tinfoil or an old piece of furniture, and he'd give them nickels and dimes. He was a nice guy, very quiet and private about his affairs. He never opened the big door or asked me to look inside the garage, and I never thought anything of it."

During the second half of 1964, months passed, and Hampton didn't appear with the rent. "I knew he must be sick or maybe dead," says Wertlieb, "and I asked my brother one day to stop by the garage. My brother came running over to the store and said, 'You should see what's going on in that garage!' I went over to look and I couldn't believe it. 'Someone oughta see this,' I told him, and I called a newspaper reporter."

A month earlier James Hampton had died of cancer in a Veterans' Administration hospital. Wertlieb was understandably concerned about the disposition of his strange inheritance. He located Hampton's only survivor, a sister in South Carolina, who didn't want anything to do with the monumental work of art. Newspaper articles brought a number of inquiries from prospective buyers. The landlord, who was awed by the beauty and magnitude of the work, wanted assurances that it would be kept intact. It was purchased by the Smithsonian Institution for a small sum of money

equal to the back rent owed. It has been exhibited at the Smithsonian, at the Abby Aldrich Rockefeller Folk Art Museum in Williamsburg, and at the Walker Art Center in Minneapolis.

The outlines of James Hampton's biography have been exhumed. He was born in 1909 in Elloree, South Carolina, the son of a Baptist minister. His formal education extended through tenth grade. He came to Washington, where he worked first as a cook, in 1939. He served in the army from 1942 to 1945 and was honorably discharged after duty in Guam. He returned to the capital and did custodial work for the General Services Administration from 1946 until his death.

People who knew him at work describe him as a quiet and reclusive man. He never married, and he had no close friends. It is thought that he had already started the construction of the Throne when he decided to rent the garage. People who came through the alley knew of his interest in scraps of gold wrapping paper and used kitchen aluminum wrap and tinfoil from cigarette and gum wrappers. It was also known that he could use old tables and chairs, burned-out light bulbs, and other unglamorous discards. He lived in a nearby furnished room and went to the garage every day directly from work and on the weekends. Although a photograph was found after his death which shows Hampton posing in front of his creation, the photographer's identity is not known. He may have been the only person invited inside the garage during Hampton's tenancy.

People who saw Hampton at his job, at his boardinghouse, in the alley outside his garage, did not consider him particularly pious. Certainly no one thought of him as either a fanatic or a madman. His landlady at the boardinghouse recalled that he'd once said he'd like to be a minister after his retirement. Examination of his writings indicates that he was inspired by electrifying visions in which God came to him and directed him in the building of the Throne. He wrote of his mystical experiences in books, signs, and tablets that are part of the construction. One inscription reads: "This is true, that the Great Moses, the giver of the 10th commandment, appeared in Washington." Another reads: "On October 21, 1946, the Star of Bethlehem appeared over our nation's capital. This is also true." Another says: "This is true that Adam, the first man God created, appeared in Person on January 20, 1949. This was on the day of President Truman's inauguration."

The central throne of the 250-piece construction rises seven feet high and is crowned by the words FEAR NOT. The architectural pieces are paired, and the entire creation is symmetrical. Pieces to the right of the throne are related to Moses and the teachings of the Old Testament, while pieces

on the left relate to the teachings of Jesus in the New Testament. There are numerous references to the mystical Book of Revelations and the Second Coming of Christ. Hampton wrote both in ordinary script and in a secret cabalistic script which, despite attempts by cryptologists, has not been deciphered. He referred to himself in governmentese as "St. James, Director of Special Projects for the State of Eternity." Perhaps he smiled at the bureaucratic title, but then again, perhaps he did not.

Like the work of other folk environmentalists, James Hampton's Throne of the Third Heaven was the result of a sustained, intense, and solitary involvement. Like other environmentalists, he worked entirely with junk and found objects. He labored by the glow of a single bulb inside the un-heated garage at night, and during the daylight hours he sat outside the door and covered light bulbs and jelly jars with foil, modeled wings to decorate his pulpits, constructed crowns and tablets, and fitted silver and gold foil over every inch of the old chairs and tables.

Most people who have studied the complex plan of the Throne feel that it was far from completion when Hampton died. His inspiration sustained him in his efforts until the end. Although it is certainly valid to speculate that the experience was all-important—the work simply intended to be an act of dedication to his God—it seems more likely that James Hampton

131

had a specific purpose in mind. Meyer Wertlieb, who has given the subject considerable thought over the years, is of the opinion that Hampton was going to start his own church in the garage when the Throne was completed. "When they set it up at the Smithsonian, they only needed a platform ten feet deep. The garage was thirty feet deep, which would have left plenty of room for chairs and for people to move around."

Wertlieb is struck by the poignancy of the magnificent effort. To him it is not an affirmation but a defeat. "Poor man," he says. "He worked day and night to realize his ambition, whatever it was. Maybe he wanted to make a name for himself in church circles. But now he's dead and it all comes to nothing. It seems to me an example of the futility of life."

Simon Rodia

"I was a poor man. Had to do a little at a time. Nobody helped me. I think if I hire a man he don't know what to do. A million times I don't know what to do myself." The pamphlet offered to visitors at the gate is short on direct quotations. "I wanted to do something in the United States because I was raised here, you understand? . . . because there are nice people in this country."

Simon Rodia, known to his Spanish-speaking neighbors as "Sam Rodilla," or as "El Italiano," or—later in his life—as "that crazy old man," was the sole creator of the famed and spectacular Watts Towers in Los Angeles, California. The Towers, which rise one hundred feet in the air, are a lace-work of glittering spires and pinnacles made of mortar encrusted with assorted flotsam and rubble: broken plates, pieces of tile, seashells, small china animals, 7-Up and Milk of Magnesia bottles. The structure has been compared to Antonio Gaudi's fantastic cathedral in Barcelona, admired both as architecture and as folk art, studied as an extraordinary feat of engineering. Although the Towers were abandoned and vandalized, and barely escaped being razed in the late 1950s, they are now considered a great cultural momument and are visited by twenty-five thousand people each year.

The soaring Watts Towers are the product of one man's grandiose imagination and fanatic perseverance. They are the creation of an artist who was obsessed with a stunning and singular fantasy and had the skill to carry it to fruition. The fact that they were almost destroyed by the abuses of vandals and the rulings of an unenlightened city building department suggests the most likely answer to the question of what happened to the work of total environmentalists of one hundred or two hundred years ago. Surely they must have existed, and yet nothing is known of their lives or their constructions. If a monument as important as the Watts Towers could have been lost in our art-conscious era, what hope must there have been for the preservation of fantastic works of art left behind by eccentrics of earlier times?

In recent years a labyrinthine seven-story, thirty-five-room house constructed over a thirty-year period by Clarence Schmidt of Woodstock, New York, was burned. "They're going to make my place a national monument," Schmidt had said, "the eighth wonder of the world." Today Schmidt is in a nursing home, and the house with its shrines and the garden with its bizarre assemblages of mirrors and found objects are desecrated ruins. James Hampton's Throne of the Third Heaven might so easily have been destroyed. Charlie Fields' polka-dotted house is weathering in an overgrown field, neglected and partially mutilated by vandals.

So let us praise and repraise the miracle on 107th Street and the Committee for Simon Rodia's Towers in Watts that has preserved it as a public treasure. As to the creator, he died in 1965, an embittered and sorrowful man, who over a decade earlier had walked away from his labor of thirty-three years under circumstances that will never be fully understood.

Simon Rodia was born in Rome in 1879 and came to this country at the age of ten or eleven. He had no formal education, but it is said that he owned and eagerly studied a set of *Encyclopaedia Britannica.* As a young man he worked in logging and mining camps and for some years as a tile setter. He also was trained as a telephone repairman. Later he came to Watts, where he purchased a small house with a good-sized lot. When he began work on the Towers, he was a forty-two-year-old widower, a small and agile man of enormous energy who sang snatches of Italian opera, drove a dashing Hudson touring car at a speed that alarmed his neighbors, and was considered a charmer and a ladies' man. The year was 1921.

In the 1920s and the 1930s Rodia's neighbors watched with wonder and delight as the spare Italian, swinging from his window washer's belt, hauling a pail of cement and a burlap bag filled with broken tiles and crockery, worked high in the air on his openwork towers. Neighborhood children brought broken plates to be set into the walls and were paid in cookies and pennies. The colorful peaks, archways, and fountains gleamed in the sunshine in the drab nighborhood of small frame houses. Rodia worked without scaffolding, without blueprints, without sketches of any

134

sort. Often he would take a day off to journey by trolley to Wilmington Beach, where he sought out particular types of seashells for special parts of his construction. He was unremittingly evasive when urged to talk about his motives for undertaking the ambitious project.

Simon Rodia's cheerful moods alternated with flashes of ill-temper and quarrelsomeness. Some days children were welcome; other days they were rejected. He permitted the members of the Pentecostal Church nearby to

135

perform baptisms by total immersion in the water basins of his fountains, and friends from the union hall drank wine with him in his garden. But at times he forbade anyone to enter his grounds. As the decades went on, he became notably irritable and despondent. He buried his Hudson touring car in the backyard. "I'm worried to death to get this work done before I leave," the aging man told a neighbor.

Rodia continued to work, and the structure grew and grew. He pressed corncobs and boot bottoms, baskets, tools, and his own fingers into the mortar to create designs. He completed the Ship of Marco Polo and the Santa Maria Tower. He embedded small cast-off china animals in the Hall of Mirrors. Earthquakes shook the area, but the ten-story tower stood firm. During World War II it was rumored that his pinnacles housed enemy radio equipment, and an increasingly uncommunicative and reclusive Simon Rodia suffered the taunts of children who sneaked into the walled garden and climbed on the towers and picked apricots from the trees.

Without warning, in 1954, Simon Rodia deeded his house and the Towers to a neighbor named Louis Sauceda who had been a boy during the early years of the construction. "I'm going away to die somewhere," he said, and he closed the door and turned his back on the work of thirty-three years and walked away. He never returned.

For five years Rodia's whereabouts were completely unknown, and then, in June 1959, he was found living in a boardinghouse in Martinez,

California, four hundred miles north of Los Angeles. He was eighty-one years old. A nephew spoke to reporters, saying only, "He wants to wash his hands of the whole thing." Later Rodia, pressed to explain his abandonment of the Towers, said, "If your mother dies and you have loved her very much maybe you don't speak of her." He remained silent and inscrutable until his death in 1965.

For four years after the owner departed, vandals assaulted the construction. Rodia's house burned down in 1957. In 1959, two men—William Cartwright and Nicholas King—bought the property from Sauceda and started seeking volunteers to repair the extensive damage. But the Los Angeles City Building Department had declared the Towers an "unsafe eyesore" and issued an order for their demolition. Protests arose from the public, from critics, artists, writers. The new Committee for Simon Rodia's Towers in Watts arranged elaborate safety tests and, with television cameras watching, the tallest tower was found to be able to withstand a pull of ten thousand pounds. The Towers, with their remarkable armature of steel rods and wire mesh, were saved.

Why did Rodia build the fantasy now known as the Watts Towers? What tragic disappointment caused him to abandon his creation? No one can answer these questions, but if it was immortality as an artist that he sought, he has achieved it.

Louis Sauceda reminisces joyously about the days when Simon Rodia was at work high in the air with his cement and his tiles. "Everybody said he was crazy," he has told reporters, "but I remember him up in the Towers singing away."

Suggestions for Further Reading

Bishop, Robert. *American Folk Sculpture*. New York: E. P. Dutton and Co., Inc., 1974.

    Authoritatively selected and lavishly illustrated.

Fuller, Edmund L. *Visions in Stone*. Photographs by Edward Weston. Pittsburgh: University of Pittsburgh Press, 1973.

    The life and work of Tennessee stone carver William Edmundson.

Gladstone, M. J. *A Carrot For a Nose: The Form of Folk Sculpture on America's City Streets and Country Roads*. New York: Charles Scribner's Sons, 1974.

    Trade signs and snowmen and the patterns on manhole covers.

Hemphill, Herbert W., Jr. and Weissman, Julia. *Twentieth Century American Folk Art and Artists*. New York: E. P. Dutton and Co., Inc., 1974.

    Most comprehensive work on twentieth-century folk art.

Janis, Sidney. *They Taught Themselves*. New York: The Dial Press, 1942.

    Early book on a large group of twentieth-century folk painters.

Larkin, David. *Innocent Art*. New York: Ballantine Books, Inc., 1974.

    Folk painting from the United States, France, Netherlands, Colombia, and other countries in Europe and in Central and South America.

Lipman, Jean. *American Primitive Paintings*. London: Oxford University Press, 1942. Dover reprint, 1972.

    Reprint of a classic.

——. *American Folk Art in Wood, Metal and Stone*. New York: Pantheon Books, Inc., 1948. Dover reprint, 1972.

    Valuable reprint.

—— and Winchester, Alice. *The Flowering of American Folk Art (1776–1876)*. New York: The Viking Press, Inc., in cooperation with the Whitney Museum of American Art, 1974.

    Handsomely produced and authoritative. Printed in conjunction with a major exhibition of folk art at the Whitney Museum.

Neal, Avon. *Ephemeral Folk Figures*. Photos by Ann Parker. New York: Clarkson N. Potter. Distributed by Crown Publishers, Inc., 1969.

    Scarecrows, snowmen, and harvest figures.

Watson, Patrick. *Fasanella's City*. New York: Ballantine Books, Inc., 1973.

    The paintings of Ralph Fasanella with the story of his life and development as an artist.

American Museums with Outstanding Folk Art Collections

EASTERN UNITED STATES

Abby Aldrich Rockefeller Folk Art Museum, Williamsburg, Virginia.

Essex Institute, Salem, Massachusetts.

Heritage Plantation, Sandwich, Massachusetts.

Marine Historical Association, Inc., Mystic Seaport, Mystic, Connecticut. (There are also Whaling Museums in Nantucket, Massachusetts, and New Bedford, Massachusetts.)

Museum of American Folk Art, 49 W. 53rd Street, New York, New York.

Museum of Appalachia, Norris, Tennessee.

National Gallery of Art (Garbisch Collection of Primitive Paintings), Washington, D.C.

New York State Historical Association, Cooperstown, New York.

Old Sturbridge Village, Sturbridge, Massachusetts.

Pennsylvania Farm Museum of Landis Valley, Lancaster, Pennsylvania.

Philadelphia Museum of Art (Pennsylvania-German collection), Philadelphia, Pennsylvania.

Shelburne Museum, Shelburne, Vermont.

Smithsonian Institution, Museum of History and Technology, Washington, D.C.

MIDWEST

Bishop Hill Heritage Association and Bishop Hill Memorial, Bishop Hill, Illinois.

Circus World Museum, Baraboo, Wisconsin.

Henry Ford Museum and Greenfield Village, Dearborn, Michigan.

Museum of Woodcarving, Spooner, Wisconsin.

Norwegian-American Museum, Decorah, Iowa.

WESTERN UNITED STATES

Museum of International Folk Art, Museum of New Mexico, Santa Fe, New Mexico.

Taylor Museum, Colorado Springs, Colorado.

140

Index

ELINOR LANDER HORWITZ has been a free-lance writer since her graduation from Smith College. She writes book reviews and features for the *Washington Star News,* has written for many national magazines, and is the author of a number of books for young and adult readers. She and her husband, neurosurgeon Norman Horwitz, live in Chevy Chase, Maryland. They have three children.

J. RODERICK MOORE has a master's degree in American Folk Culture from the Cooperstown (New York) Graduate Program. After a variety of jobs, including stints as a coal miner, an apple picker, and an apprentice gunsmith, he turned to research and teaching. Mr. Moore has served as archivist, coordinator, and consultant for numerous folk life and folk art projects and has contributed articles on related subjects to several journals. He is currently on the faculty of Ferrum College, Ferrum, Virginia, where he is Associate Director of the Blue Ridge Institute.